# ONE SOLDIER

# ONE SOLDIER

## A CANADIAN SOLDIER'S FIGHT AGAINST THE ISLAMIC STATE

DILLON HILLIER
WITH RUSSELL HILLIER

HarperCollins*Publishers*Ltd

*One Soldier*
Copyright © 2016 by Dillon Hillier and Russell Hillier.
All rights reserved.

Published by HarperCollins Publishers Ltd

First published by HarperCollins Publishers Ltd in an original trade paperback edition: 2016
This trade paperback edition: 2017

*One Soldier* is the author's real-life experience. Some names have been changed.

All photos courtesy of Dillon Hillier.

HarperCollins books may be purchased for educational, business,
or sales promotional use through our Special Markets Department.

HarperCollins Publishers Ltd
2 Bloor Street East, 20th Floor
Toronto, Ontario, Canada
M4W 1A8

*www.harpercollins.ca*

Library and Archives Canada Cataloguing in Publication
information is available upon request.

ISBN 978-1-44344-932-8

Printed and bound in the United States of America
LSC/H   10   9   8   7   6   5   4   3   2

*To the victims of the Islamic State and those who fight against them.*

—DILLON HILLIER

*To my kids. May you grow to be smart, strong and beautiful.*

—RUSSELL HILLIER

# CONTENTS

## GLOSSARY OF TERMS

FOB—forward operating base; a small military base or outpost near the front lines

IED—improvised explosive device

KRG—Kurdistan Regional Government; ruling body of the predominantly Kurdish territory in northern Iraq

NVGs—night vision goggles

PESHMERGA—the official army of the Kurdistan Regional Government

PKK—nationalist and communist-inspired Kurdish guerilla force associated with the Kurdistan Workers' Party, deemed a terrorist organization by some Western nations

SHIA—a branch of Islam whose adherents comprise the majority of the population of Iraq

YPG—Syrian version of the PKK


## LIST OF PEOPLE

GENERAL ARAZ—Peshmerga general in command of the Daquq front

PKK ALI—commander of PKK military unit in the Daquq district

LIEUTENANT ALI—Peshmerga officer and Dillon Hillier's primary contact in Kurdistan

LIEUTENANT DAN—Peshmerga officer on the Rashad front

ETHAN—Texan, former American marine and a switched-on warrior

AGGAR—second-in-command of PKK Ali's unit

BROTHAHAN—PKK fighter severely wounded at Tal al-Ward

BILAL—Peshmerga officer in General Araz's headquarters unit

ZENDE—female PKK fighter

MIKE—friend and former Canadian soldier

SHEIK JAFFER—overall commander of the Kurdish Peshmerga

AKAM—Sheik Jaffer's right-hand man

ARES—Greek god of war

ONE SOLDIER

# PROLOGUE

26 NOVEMBER 2014
TAL AL-WARD (20 KILOMETRES SOUTH OF KIRKUK)
1430 HRS

I LOOKED UP TO THE HEAVENS IN WONDER. IT WASN'T SUPPOSED to snow in this land of desert heat and sand. That's the way I had pictured Iraq since a child, and yet small white flakes falling from grey clouds left a fleeting trace of snow, which was no mirage. I had harboured the same misconception about Afghanistan, but remembered clearly how the mountain peaks surrounding Kabul were capped in white by the time the last Canadian soldiers left that desolate land. The same land Alexander the Great had surveyed from atop the Khyber Pass and concluded wasn't worth his time and effort. The same land that saw off the might of the British Empire in the nineteenth century and the conscripted soldiers of the Russian army a century later. I had been on that last deployment to Afghanistan exactly one year ago, but now I was in Iraq, fighting a very different war. The enemy, however, was the same.

Taliban, ISIS, Islamic fundamentalists, terrorists, jihadists. The list can go on, but the name doesn't really matter. In the end they belong to an evil and brutal group that needs to be put down with lethal force. That's exactly what I was in Iraq to do. I had quit my job and sold my car, and with the money I bought a one-way ticket from Canada to Kurdistan. After a flight halfway across the world, I had arrived on a personal mission to fight against the Islamic State. This was my calling. I knew that this was what I was meant to do.

The biting wind howled and my body jostled with every bump and crater in the back of the white Toyota pickup truck, bringing me back to where my mind needed to be. I wasn't sure where we were going, only that the convoy was travelling west through flat lands, where the only visible colour was a drab brown that lent an air of impoverishment to everything it touched.

Earlier that morning a man named Aggar, one of the few Kurds in the PKK unit who could speak a semblance of broken English, had said simply, "Grab your gun and a small bag."

"Where are we going and for how long?" I had asked, but Aggar had either ignored the question or didn't understand my English words. Then he jumped into a waiting vehicle, leaving me with unanswered questions. The mixed convoy of pickup trucks and SUVs loaded with Kurdish fighters had left the military base and hadn't stopped driving since.

The Kurds were keeping me in the dark during the journey, and even if the other armed men in the back of the moving truck had been willing to share any intel, there was not one of them who could speak a word of English. There was nothing else to do but wait and try to stay warm. I pulled a black toque over my ears to keep warm against the buffeting winds that made a howling noise over the exposed truck bed. Then something caught my eye.

I saw black-and-white smoke, billowing upward ahead of the truck in several columns from a sand berm that stretched as far across the landscape as a man could see. At the time, I had no idea I was looking at a line of fortifications that spans more than 1,500 kilometres across the entire width of Northern Iraq.

The truck sped forward and the eerie howl returned, but it wasn't the wind, nor was it the sound of the wild dogs that roam the bleak landscape. It was the sound of war, and for the first time ever, I had heard a Katyusha rocket scream through the air. A mobile Kurdish battery was firing the Soviet-era rockets, and they exploded wildly into jihadi-held positions that lay on the far side of a canal about half a kilometre away. Now I knew where I was. I didn't need Aggar or anyone else to tell me that I had reached the front lines in the war against ISIS.

This is what I had come to Kurdistan for. This would be a day of blood, death and tears, and as the sun set I gave a whispered thanks that I had survived the ultimate test of a man. Good men and bad were killed and wounded that day, and I added to the casualty toll. You can never forget days like this, and I did my part to fight those who serve evil.

The place was called Tal al-Ward, and this is my story.

# I.

# ONE-WAY TICKET

THERE'S MORE TO LIFE THAN THE ONE I'M LIVING. WHO AMONG us can honestly look in the mirror and not say the same? For most, it's a question we dare not ask because we fear the answer. If ever the thought intrudes upon our minds, we retreat into our daily routines, our jobs and our hobbies to pretend that we've maximized the life that's been given to us. But it's a fraudulent masquerade.

There's more to life. I knew this to be true. The thought had been gnawing at me, and now that I was alone in a prairie hotel room, I couldn't escape it. There was no longer any doubt about what I had to do, and I was tired of pretending otherwise. The only question was whether I had the guts to begin the mission I had planned.

My laptop computer was lit up on the hotel-room bed, and I forced myself to stop pacing the small room. I took a seat on the mattress and stared at the computer screen, which showed the price of a one-way ticket from Calgary to Qatar and then on to a city called Sulaymaniyah, over ten thousand kilometres away in northern Iraq. I had never heard of the city before and had no idea how to pronounce it properly when I first saw it on a map.

I should have bought the ticket already, but I was being indecisive and hated the wavering feeling. The airfare was expensive, but I had just been paid for the past two weeks of work, welding and decommissioning old potash mines on the Canadian prairies. The money was fantastic, more than I had ever made before, and for once my bank account wasn't a gaping black hole of debt. All I had to do was click once on the "confirmation of purchase" button and I would purchase the ticket that would bring me to Iraqi Kurdistan and the front lines in the battle against the Islamic State. One click and it would be done. It was all so simple, if I ignored the indisputable fact that there was a lot that could go wrong.

"A lot can go wrong" feels like an understatement when you are a Canadian flying blindly ten thousand kilometres into a war-torn country that civilization had retreated from decades ago. Exactly one year before, I had been with the Canadian army in Afghanistan, a country just as backward as Iraq, maybe more so. But at least I was part of the Canadian army in that country. There were always friends and brothers in uniform around who would watch my back, whom I could speak English to and trust with my life. But this mission was different. I would be alone. But that's what happens when you fly into Iraq by yourself to fight against the Islamic State.

The first obstacle in my path was the seemingly simple act of leaving Canada. Yet this wasn't as routine as packing a few items into a suitcase and remembering to bring my passport and toothbrush. I wasn't a twentysomething university student flying to Mexico with my bros during reading week. No, I was a former Canadian soldier flying across international borders with a bullet-proof tactical vest, helmet and military attire that would be sure to raise enough eyebrows at customs to warrant a meeting with an RCMP airport security detail. That might actually have been the best-case scenario. If I was going to get detained anywhere during my expedition to Kurdistan, it might as well be in a holding room within a Canadian airport. If I was stopped in Canada, I could at least expect a coffee and a call to a lawyer. God only knows what would happen if I was halted and detained by authorities in Qatar or Iraq. Needless to say, it wouldn't be good.

The second obstacle was the actual landing in Kurdistan, a crescent that arcs across the northern reaches of Iraq and borders on Syria, Turkey and Iran. With neighbours like these, the nine million people who call Kurdistan home can be forgiven for believing that they live in one of the most dangerous parts of the world. And that was before the emergence of ISIS. Prior to the 1991 Gulf War, the Kurdish people were subjected to chemical-weapon attacks from Saddam Hussein and were in the crosshairs of Iraqi ethnic cleansing.

Thankfully, Kurdistan has been a de facto country, free of Iraqi overlords in Baghdad, since American fighter jets started patrolling the Kurdish skies during the first Iraq War in 1991. People who love to disparage America as an imperial force of evil in the world should talk to a Kurd. They love the USA because it was American planes that stopped the genocide of their people by Saddam Hussein.

I had done my homework to verify the identities of my Kurdish contacts upon arrival, but there were still no guarantees. If the contacts weren't who they claimed to be, I might be walking into a trap. There was a real possibility that, instead of being embraced by friendly Kurdish soldiers upon arrival, I would be gunned down by ISIS agents at the baggage carousel inside the Sulaymaniyah airport. Or worse, taken for a blindfolded ride in the back of a jeep into the middle of the desert, where a masked man with a dirty black beard and long knife would be waiting for me in front of a camera mounted on a tripod.

And these were just my immediate concerns. Even if everything went smoothly, if I were able to leave Canada, if I were able to cross through Qatar to Iraq, if my contacts in Kurdistan were legit, I was leaving to fight in a war where tens of thousands had already been killed, maimed, raped and tortured via the most brutal and sickeningly creative methods imaginable: beheadings, crucifixions, impalings and being burned alive are just some of the ways that ISIS deals with its enemies. It's medieval torture reincarnated into the modern world.

There was no point trying to fool myself that death wasn't a possibility. I knew the risks and had weighed the odds. Going to Kurdistan to fight ISIS meant battles, combat and potentially death. But sometimes in life, you have to do the right thing despite the risks and dangers. That's what it means to be a man and a soldier.

I looked at the flight itinerary on my computer screen again. I would be giving up a high-paying job and a comfortable life of women, partying and excess. But in the end those things didn't matter because it wasn't the life I was meant to live. I was a soldier, and that's something that never leaves you, even when the uniform has been tucked away, folded and hidden from view. Mine was neatly ironed and hanging up in a closet in my older brother's suburban home in Calgary. I was often disgruntled with the Canadian army and had been happy to leave the forces, but I was always proud of the dark green uniform and my Princess Patricia's Canadian Light Infantry (PPCLI) regimental badge.

I remembered coming home from the last deployment to Afghanistan with my mind already made up that I would leave the army. That was one year ago. There were times at Camp Phoenix, just outside the Afghan capital of Kabul, when I would scour the Internet for jobs, dreaming of the day when I could be my own man and not take orders from anyone. I couldn't wait to let my beard grow, to wake up and go to bed whenever I wanted. Hell, I could even tie the laces on my new construction boots any damn way I wanted to. As soon as I was back in Canada, I put in for my release and started counting the days. All the sergeants and warrant officers told me I was making a terrible mistake, that I would regret leaving the army, with all of its stability, structure and routine. But of course I knew better.

"You'll be back in a year," one of my superiors warned. One year was the minimum amount of time that must pass before a soldier can re-enlist. But I scoffed at the notion. On the day of my dismissal, I addressed my platoon at the army barracks in Shilo, Manitoba. The men stood at ease. Some of them were friends, others just people that I had to work with. A few good words were said between us. I wished them all well and then was on my way after returning my kit and gear to the quartermaster. I had never felt happier than when I drove off the base, heading west on the Trans-Canada Highway towards Calgary. When the Rocky Mountains appeared on the distant horizon just east of Calgary, I smiled because there was a new life waiting and the freedom was intoxicating.

Yet the uniform becomes a part of you, a connection that gets stronger the longer you wear it. It's not just rank insignias and Velcro patches, it's an identity. A soldier is forced to test himself while in uniform; he will endure physical and emotional pain and suffering and become stronger because of it. Every soldier knows himself better because of the uniform, and so it becomes a source of strength and confidence.

The truth is that, after a few months in the civilian world, I had begun to miss the uniform and everything that goes with it. In a strange way it's like I was missing a part of myself, and with daily stories on the news of the Islamic State's signature brutality, I felt the soldier's instinct to do something and take action stirring inside.

"Fuck it," I said to myself.

I tapped my finger on the pad on the computer and bought the ticket. I felt a surge of relief, and I knew that was a sign I had made the right decision. I lit a cigarette and laid my head on a stack of pillows. Now came the hard part—telling my family.

## 14 NOVEMBER 2014
## CALGARY

"You better come see me tomorrow because I'm leaving for a while."

The text message was cryptic, but my oldest brother, Russell, knew exactly what I was saying when he read that single sentence. As far as he was concerned, I might as well have written, "I'm leaving on a suicide mission to fight against the Islamic State."

Russell waited a moment for another text, but the phone was silent and he slid it back in his pocket. He wasn't surprised by the message I had sent. The truth was that a part of him knew that this day was inevitable. Months earlier, I remember talking to my brother about ISIS rolling over the Iraqi army at Mosul, and since that time we would often talk about the current battles and actions in the newest Iraqi war. I was fresh out of the army and a member of the civilian world, but I was still keeping track of the jihadist sweep through Syria and Iraq in the summer of 2014. In the weeks and months after ISIS first started making headlines for their trademark savagery, I would often muse to close family and friends about travelling to northern Iraq to join the Kurdish army, known as the Peshmerga, to fight against the Islamic State.

*Peshmerga* is a Kurdish word that means "those who face death." It's an appropriate word because they have been facing death continuously since the summer of 2014, when the jihadi forces stormed westward out of Syria. Thousands of Peshmerga have been killed in the war, but they have proven themselves to be the only effective ground force that can stand up to ISIS and halt the advance of the Caliphate's black-and-white flags in the defence of their homeland. Russell bore the brunt of my musings, but as time went on, my talk of joining "the Pesh" became more frequent and planned out.

"I'll come by tomorrow morning," Russell texted back. He told himself that talk of my mission to fight ISIS was a phase I was going through. Surely this was a case of missing both the thrill and discipline of army life, and my crazy idea would pass soon enough. That had been his hope all along. But then the terrorist attacks in October struck close to home.

First, Warrant Officer Patrice Vincent was deliberately rammed by a vehicle and killed in Saint-Jean-sur-Richelieu, Quebec, a target of a homegrown terrorist who had converted to Islam. Two days later, Corporal Nathan Cirillo was gunned down while standing on ceremonial guard duty at the National War Memorial in Ottawa. Michael Zehaf-Bibeau was another homegrown terrorist, one with ideological ties to ISIS. After shooting Corporal Cirillo, Zehaf-Bibeau entered the Parliament Buildings with a premeditated plan to storm a Conservative caucus meeting and inflict mass casualties on the Canadian political leadership. Had he been successful, it would have easily been the deadliest political attack in Canadian history.

Patrick Brown, then a member of Parliament for Barrie and now the leader of the Ontario Progressive Conservative Party, was on Parliament Hill and in the room targeted by Zehaf-Bibeau on that day. I spoke to Brown afterward about what happened during those tense moments.

"I realized there was a gunman when we heard banging sounds in the corridor. At first I thought it might have been filing cabinets falling, but after repeated shots we all realized it was gunfire. Some ran from the room and others stayed. The former police officers in caucus really took charge of the situation. As more shots were heard and the intensity picked up, I assumed we were the target of a terrorist attack because the Prime Minister was in the room with us."

Gunfire echoed throughout the marble corridors of Parliament until Zehaf-Bibeau was taken down by Kevin Vickers, the sergeant-at-arms. Fortunately, Vickers was armed with more than the ceremonial mace of Parliament. When the attack was over, Zehaf-Bibeau's body was riddled with 9-millimetre entry holes.

After the terrorist attacks by jihadis on Canadian soil, my resolve to enter the war against ISIS hardened and there was no turning back. I grew up less than an hour's drive from Parliament Hill, so Zehaf-Bibeau's attack hit home hard. It felt like an assault on my own backyard. Dozens of Canadians such as Zehaf-Bibeau had already heeded the call to jihad and joined ISIS. I knew I had to do something against these butchers. With my unique set of military skills learned in the Canadian army, I felt that I was well positioned to help those who could not help themselves. I felt it was my duty to fight ISIS.

## 15 NOVEMBER 2014
## 1000 HRS

I met my brother the morning of my planned departure for Kurdistan at a coffee shop in Calgary, and Russell did everything short of ripping up my passport or placing a call to the RCMP to stop me. We are both strong, physical guys, and had things turned ugly it would have made for quite the scene. But Russell told me afterward that he saw in my eyes that I had made up my mind. It was the look of a man tired of reaffirming to himself the justness of his decision. Still, my brother pressed his case.

"This won't be like Afghanistan. You'll be alone with no one to help you if things go badly," he said.

"I know that." My answers are typically short. I've never been one to talk a lot, and my time in the military has only heightened my brevity. In the army, orders and commands are given with precision, using the fewest words possible so as to avoid ambiguity, and that had rubbed off on me. Even informal chats while in uniform tend to skew short.

"People respect what you did in the Canadian army and your tour in Afghanistan. No one will respect you for this. You'll be a mercenary in their eyes."

"Man, I don't give a fuck what people think." This attitude has gotten me in trouble since a young age, from teachers, parents and the law. I have to work on it.

"What if you get wounded or killed? We both know people who lost limbs in Afghanistan. Have you asked yourself if you're willing to live the rest of your life without legs or an arm for this cause?" It was a valid point. Hundreds of Canadian soldiers had been severely wounded and lost limbs in the last ten years of war in Afghanistan. I knew some of these people, so it wasn't a tangential point.

"I'll be all right, bro" was all I said.

"You say that, but when the first bullet flies, your fate is out of your hands. You can never be entirely in control in battle."

"I'll be good, bro. I got this." I had faith in my training, but you can't always hide from a sniper, or a stray bullet, or a mortar plunging from the sky. I knew this to be true, as all soldiers do. Of course there would be risks, but that is inevitable whenever you take meaningful action.

"Have you verified your contacts? The people you think of as friendlies one day might sell you off to ISIS the next. You could land in Kurdistan and then be driven into the desert and killed. There's a hundred ways for this to end badly, ways that you can't even imagine."

I shared the worry that I was walking into a trap. "I've thought about that. It's definitely a possibility, but a small one." Flying into Sulaymaniyah, Kurdistan, was a risk, but a calculated one that I felt was worth taking.

Russell changed tack and began playing on guilt. "This will take years off of Mom and Dad's lives. I don't know if Mom can handle it." Of all the things my brother could have said, this is the one that stung most, because it was true. It gave me pause, but it's not like I hadn't already thought about it. For a mother, what could be worse than having a son in harm's way? She had already worried and stressed while I was in Afghanistan, and I hated the thought of making her go through it again. Only this time, her fears would be heightened and more justified because the mission was much more dangerous.

"I have to do this. I can't explain it. I just have to go and help these people. If I can save just one life in Iraq, it will be worth it. I want people to be happy for me that I'm doing what I know is right." I genuinely believed those words. There were people who needed my help: Kurds, Yazidis and Christians; women, children and men too old to fight. I would have been ashamed to sit back and watch the atrocities happen on TV from the comfort of my couch, knowing that I could have acted in some small way to stop it.

That was it. I was going and there was nothing Russell could do to stop me. He put his hands to his face and sighed deeply. He had tested my commitment and exhausted all efforts to persuade me, but I never doubted that in the end he would do everything possible to support and help me in my mission. He's bailed me out of trouble when I needed help so many times, and he would again. I'm lucky to have a brother like him.

I wrote down the usernames and passwords for my Facebook page, email and online banking on a piece of paper and handed it to Russell. If ISIS captured me, they would love to use my social media accounts for propaganda purposes. Russell was in charge of making sure the passwords were changed if needed so that this wouldn't happen.

"Tell me how this is going to work. You land in Kurdistan, and what happens next?" he asked.

A safe insertion into Kurdistan was Russell's biggest concern, and one that I shared. But I had an answer and began to explain the murky world of foreign recruitment into the fight against the Islamic State.

‡‡‡

IN LATE SEPTEMBER 2014 I HAD BEGUN SERIOUSLY DIGGING INTO the logistics of what I needed to do to join the fight against ISIS. It seems so pedestrian and amateur, but my first action was to make a post to a Peshmerga Facebook page, an act I assumed would amount to nothing. I was wrong.

I wrote that I was a Canadian veteran who wanted to join the fight against the Islamic State, and shortly after a guy named Ken replied to my post, claiming to know someone who could help. I never heard from Ken again, but I did hear from a woman who called herself Kerry Dragon, a private contractor operating in Kurdistan, who created a closed Facebook group with only seven invitees. There was a Peshmerga officer named Lieutenant Ali, me, a Swede of Kurdish background, and four Americans, including Ethan, a former American marine. All the Westerners had military training, which was exactly what Lieutenant Ali was looking for. Dragon's real name is a mystery to me; in fact, I don't even know with 100 per cent certainty that she even exists. I know her only as a Facebook profile.

Lieutenant Ali was recruiting soldiers into a Peshmerga unit comprised of Western volunteers with military experience. Hundreds of people have left Europe and North America to join ISIS, and it seemed the Kurds had figured out that they should start playing the same game. Having a team of trained veterans from the West on the front would be a significant localized advantage for them. Our presence would also help nullify the effect of the Western jihadi scum who had flocked to the Caliphate. In my opinion, one Western volunteer is worth at least ten bearded jihadis on the battlefield, so maybe we could help even the odds.

Over the days and weeks, I talked to Lieutenant Ali and he told me everything I wanted to hear—mainly that I would be on the front lines as much as possible, with no shortage of trigger time on the enemy. We corresponded over Facebook, with Lieutenant Ali providing pictures and articles about himself in the Kurdish media to prove his legitimacy.

"I can't be 100 per cent about him," I admitted to my brother, "but I have a friend who has checked into him."

"Who? Mike?"

I nodded my head. It's not his real name, but Mike was a former soldier, a parachutist who had been among the first Canadians to drop into Afghanistan after the 9/11 terrorist attacks. When I told Mike about my plans to travel to Iraq, he sprang into action and began plumbing his contacts in the region, looking for intelligence on Lieutenant Ali. Yet the search for information on the Peshmerga officer didn't turn up any results. It was true that my faith in Lieutenant Ali was a gamble, but then so was the entire plan. At the end of the day, my mission wasn't going anywhere without the help of local, on-the-ground contacts. I had to trust someone, so it might as well have been Lieutenant Ali.

With the Americans showing interest on Kerry Dragon's Facebook group, at least there was the prospect that I wouldn't be the lone Westerner in Kurdistan. Even having just one other companion to speak with would make a huge difference while operating in a foreign land.

The other members of the group and I communicated often and began hashing out our plans. We would talk on Skype and Facebook every few nights and discuss logistics. One guy claiming to be an American soldier was a fraud and I called him out on it. I could tell by the way he spoke that he had never worn a uniform. He was lost with our use of military jargon and his dishonesty was easily exposed. The others were genuine, though. They felt the same way I did, that we had certain skill sets we could use to help people in need.

We ex-soldiers who would form the nucleus of Lieutenant Ali's unit of foreign volunteers talked about the immediate concern of a safe insertion into Iraq and the tools and resources required to sustain a long-term mission. We had to do a lot of logistical planning before we left our homes. We developed a list of military gear that we would need to prosecute our fight against ISIS, which included items such as camo uniforms, tactical vests, knives, Kevlar helmets, combat boots, bags and packs that we could bring from North America. Other items, such as our guns, ammunition, optics and range finders, we would have to pick up in country at an arms market because they are restricted from civilian use and transport.

We also began working on our standard operating procedures (SOPs). Every professional fighting force has SOPs that govern everything from training, communication and chain of command to prisoner treatment and combat. I hoped we would be the core of what would become a larger unit of foreign volunteers, and we wanted to be completely professional in our conduct. Our SOPs would reflect this.

Should we arrive in Kurdistan separately or as a group? This was one of the first questions we had to resolve. Both options carried risks and merit. On the one hand, there is safety in numbers, lending credence to the notion that all of us should arrive in Kurdistan on the same flight. However, if ISIS were to be tipped off to our arrival, there could be a massacre of Western infidels in the Sulaymaniyah airport, a propaganda victory that ISIS would love.

Separate insertions certainly reduced the chance of mass casualties. If ISIS did know about the arrival of Western volunteers

augmenting Kurdish forces, only the first man would be killed—
or, worse, captured. But if everything went well, the first arrival
could help pave the way for the others, leading to a smoother
transition. That was the plan our small group agreed to. The next
question was who would be the first to go. I had the answer.

THAT NIGHT IN THE SASKATCHEWAN HOTEL ROOM, I TOOK A
screenshot of my plane ticket and emailed it to the crew. There
had been enough talk; it was time to take action. The other members of the clandestine group vowed to do the same, but who
knew who was serious and who was not. There were the usual
reasons why they couldn't buy tickets right away, most of them
financial, and they started backing away. I didn't fault the other
veterans for not following me and buying their airline tickets
more promptly. After all, packing up for a dangerous mission
to Iraq is a grave decision, one that demands that you put your
affairs in order. Still, their hesitation created a lingering thought
that I would not only be the first volunteer to fight ISIS, but I
might be the only one.

On the evening of November 15, I said goodbye to my friends
in Calgary, not knowing if I would see them again. "Stay safe and
keep your head on a swivel" was the common refrain. "I love you,
bro. Come home safe" were the last words Russell said to me
before I left.

A friend drove me to the airport, and I made my way to the
British Airways kiosks. All of my bags were packed with military
paraphernalia, but I checked them the same way a tourist going
on vacation would. Passage through airport screening went easily enough and I made my way to the terminal. *So far so good*, I

thought, but I was still nervous and fully expecting a visit from airport security at any moment. It never came, and with five minutes left before I boarded my flight, I made the final edits on an email to my parents, who had no idea what I was about to do.

I had thought about telling my family a lie, that I was going on vacation in Thailand for six months, but decided against it. It would do no good. Word would get out. Instead I came clean with my plan . . . sort of.

**15 NOVEMBER 2014**
**1908 HRS**

*Subject: Departing*

*I am minutes away from boarding a flight to Sulaymaniyah Iraqi Kurdistan. There I will be helping train Kurdish Peshmerga in their fight against ISIS. I intend on staying well away from the front. Sulaymaniyah is 200km from the front.*

This part wasn't true. I would be on the front lines, and wouldn't have it any other way, but I couldn't bring myself to say as much. My dad probably wouldn't believe the ruse anyway, but it was worth a shot.

*Keep an eye on the National Post; late next week Stew Bell should be writing a story about what I am doing. Now as far as what you should tell mom I am not sure. It's your call. This is what I was meant to do dad. I was just lying to myself and telling myself that I enjoyed my work. It was all bullshit. I will be in touch as much as possible. Don't freak if you don't hear from me for a few days. Anyway take care. I love you and I love mom. This is my calling. This is what I have to do.*

*Cheers,*

*Dillon*

My dad is an elected Canadian politician with access to channels of political power and the people who could have prevented—or at least delayed—my departure for Kurdistan. But with only five minutes left, there was no time for him to react or make the phone calls that could have derailed my plans.

I boarded the plane, sure of my mission and pretty damn sure what my family would think. I knew they would be crushed by the email. I just hoped that they would come to understand eventually why I had made this decision. Too many Canadians had left cities like Montreal, Ottawa, Calgary and Edmonton to do the wrong thing in Iraq and Syria, to butcher and rape innocents and spread their Islamic Caliphate across the world. These are people who had every advantage in life, yet chose to walk down a dark path. I felt I had a duty, a calling, to even the score with these traitors. If I came across a Canadian or Western jihadist while in Iraq, I wouldn't hesitate to pull the trigger.

The known risks were many, the unknown risks even more numerous, but as the engines roared and the plane lifted from the ground, the journey had begun. I had some answers, but in my heart even I knew there was a lot that could go wrong. But sometimes you have to go for it. I was going to fight the Islamic State, and there was no turning back.

# 2.

# ARRIVAL IN KURDISTAN

**17 NOVEMBER 2014**
**SULAYMANIYAH, KURDISTAN**
IMAGINE YOURSELF LYING IN BED, TRYING TO SLEEP, BUT NOT being able to. You look at the clock to see what time it is and realize that there is only a few hours of darkness left before you have to wake up for work, which only makes things worse. I've had those nights—we all have—but they were nothing compared to what I was feeling on the long flight to Iraq. My mind was racing with so many thoughts and emotions, and it wouldn't stop. I tried to slow it all down with a couple of rye and gingers, but that strategy didn't work. The drinks made me drowsy, but I still couldn't sleep. The excitement and worry of my mission was all-encompassing, and all I wanted to do was feel the plane land and jump out of my seat. Yet that was still several hours away. My mind wandered to all kinds of strange places and scenarios that might greet me upon arrival at the airport, but after a while I couldn't think about my fate anymore. For some reason my thoughts were now turned to

Afghanistan and the last Canadian army deployment to that war-stricken country.

While on the plane to Kurdistan, I remembered being on the army base in Shilo, Manitoba, and hearing my former commanding officer saying, "We're going in hot." That line had hit me like a lightning bolt. "Going in hot" meant arriving in Afghanistan fully geared up for battle. Weapons, ammo, combat gear, all the trappings of war would be in place for the landing in Kabul. Clearly, the words had come as somewhat of a surprise to the rest of the battalion—the soldiers began murmuring quietly among themselves. By 2013 the heavy fighting in Kandahar and Panjwaii District was supposed to be a thing of the past, and the last Canadian deployment was supposed to be a low-key mission, mainly training the Afghan National Army, guarding the embassy and conducting convoy duty around Kabul. The men joked that we were there to "burn down the shitters."

I had hoped that our mission wouldn't be as dull as everyone expected, that the Canadians would be preparing for danger and that the enemy might be ready. That's exactly what I had wanted. I didn't want to be in Afghanistan winding down the clock and sitting uselessly on a NATO base. I wanted to get at the enemy jihadists. That is why I had joined the army in the first place.

I was only thirteen when Osama bin Laden and al-Qaida took down the twin towers in the September 11 terrorist attacks. But that attack changed the Canadian army. The era of blue helmets and United Nations peacekeeping missions was over. The rise of Islamic terrorism meant that the Canadian army would now be an instrument of war and combat.

Unfortunately, I missed out on an earlier deployment to Afghanistan because of a severe beating I took in Edmonton. To this day I'm not sure what happened. I can only remember walking down a city street and then waking up in a hospital bed with a smashed jaw and a broken forearm that were both fixed with the help of metal plates that will hold my bones together for the rest of my life. The police told me it's not uncommon for soldiers to be attacked on Edmonton streets, and they never found the culprits. Regardless, I was unable to train for that deployment and was transferred to a different battalion within the PPCLI. I thought I had missed my opportunity to be part of the Afghanistan mission, and I was thankful when word came down the chain of command that my battalion would be the last Canadian unit deployed to that country.

Training in the lead-up to our deployment was extensive, everything from combat first aid to target practice and spotting improvised explosive devices. IEDs were the scourge of the Canadian army in Afghanistan and accounted for many deaths and maimings. They were the Taliban's weapon of choice once they realized that they couldn't stand up to our soldiers in pitched combat. IEDs are basically homemade bombs that any villager with a bit of training can make. All you need is a vessel that can hold explosive material, a detonation device and a willingness to set the charge. The Taliban were notorious for burying IEDs along paths and roadways, and of the 158 Canadians killed in that war, the vast majority were killed by these homemade bombs. I heard of one scenario where a NATO soldier stepped out of his armoured vehicle and planted his feet directly onto a buried IED. He was killed in the explosion.

To counter the IED threat, we practiced our "five and twenties," which meant before we stepped off a vehicle, we first scanned the ground in a five-metre radius for any disturbance in the earth that might indicate a buried IED. An explosion within five metres was essentially a death sentence. If the immediate surroundings were clear, then we would do an additional scan of a twenty-metre radius around our position, as a blast in this zone would be severely debilitating, if not lethal.

The reality of the Afghanistan mission didn't quite match the training we received. My six months in country were primarily composed of garrison, convoy and sentry duty, which meant a lot of sitting around. However, I saw some terrible things in Afghanistan that still haunt me at night, but the seek-and-destroy operations where NATO troops would actively look for and engage the enemy were over, and contrary to what we had been told prior to leaving Canada, we were winding down the clock.

Most people I know who served in Afghanistan never saw the enemy, and yet we lost a lot of good soldiers in that war. The experience of coming under attack and not returning fire is embittering and demoralizing. The Afghan campaign was unfulfilling for me. I returned to Canada feeling that a lot of unfinished business had been left on the table, and I would be lying if I said that the feeling didn't contribute in some way to my decision to fight ISIS. I knew that this war would be different. On the front lines in Iraq, I would finally get a chance to see the enemy. Somewhere far below the aircraft, the jihadis were waiting for me. Their black-and-white flags would be fluttering in the winter winds, and I couldn't wait to get at them.

FROM THE PLANE'S SMALL WINDOW I COULD SEE A SICKLY brown landscape stretching outward as far as I could see. It was flat and without character, except for small patches and strips of green, oases in the Iraqi desert. *Why would anyone fight over this desolate land?* The landscape made the Canadian prairies look verdant and lush in comparison and I wondered why anyone would live here. Yet history has a way of placing people in all corners of the world, even barren wastelands like the one I was looking down at. My knowledge of history also told me that I was looking at what once was the "fertile crescent," the apparent cradle of civilization, where man's earliest societies were nurtured by the Tigris and Euphrates Rivers.

Nine thousand metres below was where the ancient kingdoms of Babylon and Mesopotamia once stood and where King Hammurabi enacted the first known codified law over three thousand years ago. The law covered such offences as striking your father, theft, assault, false accusations and what happens when your ox fatally gores somebody. Unfortunately for the guilty parties, Hammurabi's punishments typically took the form of a variety of physical mutilations or death. "An eye for an eye" is probably the best known of Hammurabi's prescriptions for dealing with crime and punishment.

It's safe to say that the law has come a long way since this ancient time, at least in the Western world. We don't hew off the hands of thieves or use knives to cut notches out of people's brows for false testimony. But what's profoundly striking is how little crime and punishment has changed in Iraq over the past three thousand years. When compared to law and order under the Islamic Caliphate, Hammurabi's code is a weak-kneed liberal document. The great kingdoms of mankind may have started in this land, but make no mistake, much of modern Iraq is a country that civilization as I know it retreated from long ago.

As the plane moved north, the land began to change. Tinges of green began overlaying the brown, arid base, and contours in the land could be seen. Then came rolling hills, and after that, mountains tipped with white snow. This was the land of the Kurds, which they've inhabited for thousands of years. The land has made them a tough people—and they need to be, considering the threats on their borders.

My ears popped as the plane made its descent into Kurdistan, and my blood was pumping. Excitement, doubt and fear rushed through my mind, and when the wheels of the plane rumbled over the tarmac, the craziness of my mission hit me.

I released the seat belt and made my way for the exit, leaving behind a tattered copy of Hemingway's *For Whom the Bell Tolls* that I had picked up in a used bookstore in Calgary. I saw similarities between my own cause and Hemingway's story about an American volunteer fighting the Spanish Civil War.

In the 1930s, hundreds of Canadians and Americans volunteered to fight the fascists in Spain. They had no support from the government in their fight against evil, but they risked their lives all the same. I felt like I was doing the same, only the enemy wasn't German-backed fascists in Spain, but Islamic jihadists in Iraq. The North American volunteers, like Hemingway, were on the losing side of the Spanish Civil War, but they had manned up and done the right thing. Compared to Spain in the 1930s, the cause I had volunteered for was just as worthy, if not more so, and travel was easier. I truly expected and hoped that history would repeat itself, that the men of my generation would follow the example set by those who joined the international brigades in Spain. Ideally, I would be just the first Western-trained veteran among hundreds who would eventually join the fight against ISIS.

I tried finishing the book while in the air, but it was futile. I had too much on my mind. I was reading the words but not piecing anything together and simply going through the motions, flipping pages.

When the plane touched down, I followed the line of dis-
embarking passengers to the baggage carousel and looked for
Lieutenant Ali, who was supposed to pick me up. I had never met
the Peshmerga officer in person, but we had talked on Skype and
I was sure I would be able to spot him. But he was nowhere to be
seen. It's times like this when you realize that a picture is only a
fraction of how we recognize people. Size, posture, gait and a host
of other mannerisms can never be properly conveyed in a picture,
and without these markers, the men in the airport terminal started
looking the same to me. Without Lieutenant Ali, I knew that I
would be walking around blind in a foreign land.

Though there were a couple of other white faces in the airport,
I was the only young man and I felt like a target. In the back of my
mind I wondered if ISIS had been tipped off to my arrival and was
waiting for me. There were people I didn't really know who knew
about my arrival, and any one of them could have passed the word
on to ISIS for financial gain. That's how kidnappings happen. I tried
to keep an eye on my surroundings, but if ISIS was going to get me
here, there wasn't much I would be able to do about it.

There were Peshmerga soldiers in the airport, and I could feel
their eyes on me. I looked back at them, studying their faces, trying
to spot the lieutenant. When the bags started arriving, one of the
Peshmerga soldiers approached. He looked to be in his thirties and
had the trappings and accoutrements of an officer.

"Dillon?" he asked in a thick accent, and then extended his
hand before I had a chance to answer. "I'm here to pick you up."

"Where's Lieutenant Ali?" I asked.

"He couldn't make it. He sent us instead." The soldier motioned
to three other uniformed men who stood off to the side, watching
us. They had side arms, rifles and camo-patterned uniforms.

*Fuck.* Already my plans for a smooth insertion into Kurdistan had been dashed. My single greatest fear was that I would not meet Lieutenant Ali and would be taken at the airport by unknown people and then turned over to ISIS. This is exactly how it would happen. But what could I do? Some things were out of my hands, and trusting the right people was one of them. I had to have some faith or else there would be no mission. That's one of the inherent risks of being the first to travel to fight a war in a foreign country. At least the men waiting for me had uniforms and looked like legitimate soldiers.

They cleared me through customs, grabbed my bags and then loaded them into a white Toyota pickup truck, the workhorse of this desert war. Without Lieutenant Ali, I was uncomfortable getting into the truck and felt defenceless. I wished that I had managed to at least conceal a knife on my person as a last resort should things go badly, but I had had no opportunity. Throughout the rest of my mission, I never repeated that mistake.

The airport was just outside of the city of Sulaymaniyah, and I knew the Peshmerga base was somewhere close by. As the truck rolled down the highway, I had no idea if we were travelling in the right direction. For all I knew, we were headed for the front, where a group of bearded jihadis would be waiting for me. But when the truck sped into the city, I felt a bit of relief. If things were going to go badly, I figured it would happen in a remote part of the countryside rather than an urban setting.

SULAYMANIYAH IS A SPRAWLING CITY OF ABOUT ONE AND A HALF million people, hemmed in by mountains and hills on all sides, by far the biggest urban centre in northeastern Iraq. An uprising in 1991 during the Gulf War expelled the Iraqi forces of Saddam Hussein from the city, as well as from the Kurdish capital of Erbil and all the other major towns in between. The creation of an American no-fly zone during the 1990s acted as a shield against Iraqi aggression, and Kurdistan was given the space it needed to evolve into a de facto state. I don't think you can find a place in the world that loves America, Texas and both George Bushes more than Kurdistan.

As we drove through the city I tried to take everything in. It's a Kurdish city, but the Western influences are everywhere, especially the Western style of clothes and fashion. The way ISIS sees it, Kurdistan is a stain of Western liberalism that has to be wiped off the map, and if the Peshmerga defences should ever fall, the jihadis would take pleasure in raping and pillaging their way through the twisting streets of this city. I chose to fight for Kurdistan for the very reasons that ISIS wants to eliminate it, and it angered me that so many of my own countrymen had chosen to join the side of evil. There were several Muslims and recent converts from Calgary, and even someone from a small town only an hour's drive from where I grew up, who had volunteered to fight under the black-and-white banners of the Caliphate. Even though my own government stated that my mission was the wrong course of action, I felt it was my duty to even the score on the people who turned their backs on Canada and everything it stood for.

It was only when the truck pulled up to the sprawling Peshmerga military base that I knew with certainty that I was safe. I'm sure my sigh of relief was audible when we drove through the manned checkpoint and parked the vehicle. As soon as I got out, Kurdish soldiers started coming from all directions to shake my hand and to take pictures with me. Only moments before, I had been worried about getting my head cut off in the desert, and now I was being feted as a hero, even though I hadn't done anything besides showing up. What a difference half an hour makes! From my very first day on the ground in Kurdistan, I was treated with a hospitality and gratitude rarely seen in Canada. The Kurdish soldiers knew that I didn't have to be there and that I had chosen to fight alongside them. More than once I heard them lament that more of the Kurdish diaspora hadn't done the same, but it's hard to fault a man for not wanting to fight a brutal enemy like ISIS.

Four Peshmerga soldiers brought me into an office full of high-ranking officers in uniform. It was clearly a place where planning and logistics got done, with maps covering the walls and paperwork strewn over wooden desks. The men with stars on their shoulders and braided cuffs dropped what they were doing when I entered and embraced me with big smiles and offered cold water and soda. To say that they were happy to see a Westerner who had come to help fight against ISIS was an understatement. At that time, the war against ISIS was very much in doubt. The jihadis had made stunning territorial gains during the summer months, routing the Iraqi national army and even pushing back the Kurdish Peshmerga in a surprise offensive. The Kurds had managed to stabilize their lines after heavy fighting and with the help of American-led air strikes, but it was clear that my arrival was a boost for their morale. Without question, the soldiers on base thought and hoped I would be the first of many trained Westerners who would help their cause. I certainly shared that hope.

The officers in the room could speak English and were easy to talk to. This was the exception in Kurdistan. I had done my research before leaving Canada and knew right from the beginning that communicating with the Kurds would be a constant challenge. Historically, Kurdistan has been a remote part of the world and was cut off from English or European influences. It's not a cosmopolitan place, and the vast majority of its people have little or no knowledge of the English language. We could communicate most of the time using hand gestures and body language to get basic points across, but for more in-depth communication, we needed smartphones. Using Facebook on our phones, the Kurds and I were able to use Google Translate to decipher messages and understand each other throughout the length of my mission. My phone was not only a lifeline to the outside world, but also a mobile translator and interpreter.

However, these officers are part of a growing number of Kurds who have Western educations and can speak English. The creation of a no-fly zone in the early 1990s, after Saddam Hussein was defeated in the Gulf War, opened Kurdistan up to the West in terms of both business and culture. A lot of the high-ranking Peshmerga commanders can speak English with varying degrees of fluency.

One of the officers gave me an Esse cigarette, which seemed to be the brand of choice in Kurdistan, and a light. "You need to get rid of this," he said, patting his cheeks while I exhaled the smoke. Like a fool, I had let my beard grow before leaving Canada because I assumed that everyone in the Middle East had one and that facial hair would help me fit in. I was wrong. "Only terrorists have beards," the officer said. It was another example of how the Kurds have adopted Western customs. In the Peshmerga, you might see thick and dark mustaches, but never a beard, just as you wouldn't in the Canadian army. I was starting to appreciate the Kurds more and more with every minute. That afternoon, the razor came out and the beard came off.

I was shown to my quarters, a large room that belonged to Lieutenant Ali. I stashed my bags and changed out of my civvies into a green Peshmerga camo uniform. But I wore my PPCLI beret and cap badge, as well as a small Velcro red-and-white Canadian flag on my breast so that my regiment and country were proudly visible and represented in the fight against ISIS. On my shoulder patch there was an embroidered Kurdish flag—a red, white and green tricolour with a sunburst in the middle. The red symbolizes the blood of those who have died for the country. Green represents the colour of the countryside. White is the colour of peace. The sunburst stands for life. It's sometimes referred to as the "colourful flag," and it's a stark contrast to the menacing black-and-white flag of ISIS. Flags are important symbols that send visual messages of who a people are and what they believe in. The brutality and savagery of ISIS exude from their flag deliberately, and the message they are sending the world is clear.

THE PESHMERGA BASE AT SULAYMANIYAH IS LARGE, WITH THOUsands of soldiers and countless compounds, barracks, depots, vehicle yards and buildings. I was shown around and took in as much as I could until Lieutenant Ali showed up later that evening. He was tall, especially by Kurdish standards, and around the same age as I was, with thick, closely buzzed black hair. Ali had been a translator for the American army, and so there was no problem talking to him.

"Sorry about not being at the airport," he said. "I just got back from Jalulu." I didn't tell him that I had been shitting bricks the entire time I was in the truck with the four strange soldiers he had sent in his place. Jalulu is a city north of Baghdad and was at the centre of some of the heaviest fighting taking place along the front. Ali was an intelligence officer and his unit was currently stationed there, but he had managed to get away from the front for a little bit.

"It's crazy down there. Lots of fighting, but we are pushing Daesh back." *Daesh*, from what I understand, is a derogatory term and acronym for ISIS that is commonly used in the Middle East. Some politicians in the West tried to adopt the term when talking about ISIS, but it never really caught on.

"But then there are the Shia militias that we have to deal with, too, and they are just as bad as ISIS." The lieutenant had just finished a brief account of what was happening in Jalulu, and from everything I saw in Iraq, Ali's description of the Shia was pretty accurate.

The war in Iraq is such a muddled mess of competing factions that it's hard to get a solid grip on the power dynamics of the region. The Shia are a branch of Islam and make up the majority of the Iraqi Arab population. It's fair to say that they are an arm's-length ally of the West in the fight against ISIS, but it's an alliance of convenience, more of a "the enemy of my enemy is my friend" kind of partnership. When Shia militias liberate towns and cities from ISIS control, the dogs of war are let loose on the populace and they can't be called back. Atrocities in a similar vein to those committed by ISIS regularly occur.

And yet, the reality is that the fight against ISIS can't be won without the Shia. Their fighters are vast in number and are backed up by Iran because they share a faith in the same branch of Islam. In fact, the Shia militias are so powerful that the central Iraqi government will one day have a hard time reeling them in.

DILLON HILLIER with RUSSELL A. HILLIER

But beyond the Shia, there are a multitude of other groups involved in the war. In the north, Christian militias and Yazidis are allied with the Kurdish Peshmerga in the fight against ISIS. In the south, there is the inept Iraqi national army, which the Americans have tried in vain to mould into an effective fighting force. There are also Iranian advisors and soldiers on the ground, embedded with the Shia.

Sunni Arabs make up the second-largest demographic group and were favoured by Saddam Hussein during his reign of terror. In the Western reaches of Iraq, Sunnis are primarily allied with ISIS, yet in some other regions they are fighting *against* ISIS. In addition, there is a sprinkling of Western special forces and volunteers like me operating in the region. And how could I forget the PKK, the Kurdish guerilla fighters who have come down from their mountain training camps to do battle with the Caliphate?

These are just the groups and factions in Iraq. It's muddled and confusing enough, but if you take into account the overlapping war in Syria and all the factions in that failed country—al-Nusra, al-Qaida, government forces, Russians, the YPG and the Syrian rebel army, to name just a few—the entire region starts looking like a dog's breakfast. It's like a game of Risk with fifty different players, except the stakes are much higher.

I DROVE WITH ALI TO A GOVERNMENT BUILDING IN SULAYMANIYAH so that I could get the paperwork for my visa sorted out. My original intention was to stay in Kurdistan for at least a year. I knew the war wouldn't be over by then, but at least it would keep me in theatre long enough to feel like I had done my part in battling

ISIS. I told myself that after twelve months I could reevaluate my situation and determine whether I should leave or stay longer. Yet the longest I could get a visa to stay in the country legally was for three months at a time. That wasn't long enough for me. Three months seemed like too short a time to actually make a difference and achieve what I had set out to do.

"Don't worry, we'll get it sorted out later," Ali said. Later. Tomorrow. In a bit. Don't worry about it. The Kurds are experts at putting a problem on the shelf in the hope that it goes away.

"Also, you coming to Jalula with me is going to have to wait. I haven't gotten permission from my commander yet to have you on the front lines."

"What the fuck, Ali?" I said.

As far as I knew, everything had already been set up and cleared for me to be at the front in an active unit. But as I was the first Western volunteer with the Peshmerga, there were a lot of grey areas in the Kurdish chain of command that both Lieutenant Ali and I had to navigate.

"What the fuck, man?" It bore repeating. "If I'm only here for three months, I need to get into a combat unit *now*."

"Don't worry, don't worry," he responded. There were those words again. The lieutenant said he would see what he could do, but with only a three-month visa, I didn't want to waste all my time at the base when I could be fighting. With only a three-month visa and no guarantee that it would be renewed, I felt compelled to get to the front as soon as possible.

I believed Lieutenant Ali when he said he would do everything possible to get me to the front quickly, but I decided to take some initiative and not wait for a posting to fall into my lap. When we got back to the Peshmerga base, I fired up my computer and made contact through the secret Facebook group with the Kurdish Swede, who I knew had contacts with the PKK. The PKK are Kurdish guerilla fighters who have a long history fighting for Kurdish independence. Turkey and Iran hate the PKK, the Kurdistan Regional Government distrusts them, and the West has labelled them as terrorists. In short, the PKK is full of unsavoury characters. However, they are also key players in the fight against ISIS, and because they are unrestrained by government and international diplomacy, attaching myself to them offered an immediate chance to see combat against ISIS, and that's what I wanted most.

The Kurdish Swede got back to me with the message that his contacts in the PKK were keen to take me on board and that there was a guarantee of seeing action with them. Excellent. This was an opportunity. I broached the subject of joining the PKK with Lieutenant Ali, at least until I got clearance with the Peshmerga chain of command to get placed in a front-line unit. He immediately tried to talk me out of it. "You won't like it. The PKK are bad people that can't be trusted." He didn't say I wouldn't be safe with them, but he implied it. Still, I had travelled around the world to fight ISIS, and with a compressed timeline, the PKK offered the best chance of fulfilling my goal. However, actually joining the PKK wasn't as simple as walking up to a recruitment station and signing my name onto a piece of paper. The secretive nature of the organization ensured that making contact was a clandestine affair. No doubt the Peshmerga brass would take a giant shit on Lieutenant Ali if they realized he was introducing me to these people.

From the Kurdish Swede, I had a name and an address for a guy I'll call PKK Ali (there are a lot of Alis in Kurdistan), and

Lieutenant Ali and I went to meet him. When we got to the house I was searched and briefly interrogated.

"You still want to go through with this?" Lieutenant Ali asked. I wasn't sure of the answer, but I felt like I couldn't turn back now. The PKK escorted us to another safe house in Sulaymaniyah, where about a dozen PKK fighters were hanging out. They looked rougher than the Peshmerga soldiers on base, and their stoic demeanour left no doubt that these guys were battle-tested. PKK Ali emerged from another room and greeted us warmly. If I chose to join these guys, he would be my commander. He seemed courteous, but there was definitely something unnerving about the middle-aged man. Maybe that's a feeling that comes from knowing he belonged to a designated terrorist organization. With Lieutenant Ali acting as interpreter, I was told that this unit of PKK would be leaving for the front near Kirkuk in a couple of days. There would be fifty of them and they would be happy to have me join.

"And I'll be free to leave whenever I want?"

"Yes, yes," said the PKK commander in English.

We made arrangements, and two days later I was riding in the backseat of a truck with Lieutenant Ali to a small PKK compound just outside of Kirkuk.

"Are you communist?" Lieutenant Ali asked me.

"No," I scoffed. I hated communism.

"These guys are. Just go along with it. And don't think of touching their women. All their fighters are celibate."

"Yeah, yeah." I had done my research and knew this already. Still, the lieutenant was worried because, if anything happened to me, his chain of command would come down hard on him. As far as the Peshmerga were concerned, Lieutenant Ali was responsible for me, and they didn't want the bad press that would come from a Canadian veteran being killed or declared MIA in the war against ISIS.

"You have my number. I'll check in with you, but call or text me if there is ever a problem."

# 3.

# IN BAD COMPANY

IT WASN'T MUCH OF A BASE—JUST A REMOTE CLUSTER OF dilapidated homes. But it was very close to the front, only about four hundred metres from a low earthen berm that stretched across the barren landscape, marking Kurdistan's frontier with ISIS. The enemy-controlled territory was about a kilometre past this low protective wall of dirt, and it was here at the PKK base that I first saw the infamous black-and-white flags of the Islamic Caliphate, just visible without binoculars in the distance, and something stirred in my soul because I knew what those banners symbolized.

When Lieutenant Ali and I stepped into the main building of the PKK forward operating base (FOB), a two-storey house, it was all hugs and smiles from PKK Ali and his men, yet I could see that the lieutenant was still skeptical. "I'll be in Jalula for a while," he told me right before leaving. "Remember to call if you need anything."

Since my arrival in Kurdistan, the Peshmerga had treated me like an officer and an independent volunteer not under the Kurdish chain of command. In other words, I had privileges and was free to come and go as I saw fit. I soon realized that the PKK didn't share this notion. As soon as Lieutenant Ali's truck pulled away, the PKK's congeniality started going sideways. The smiles disappeared just as Lieutenant Ali's white Toyota vanished into a cloud of Iraqi dust.

I sensed the change in attitude and busied myself by organizing and checking my belongings and making sure that everything I needed would be readily accessible for when the time came to head for the front.

There is no indoor plumbing in this part of Iraq, and so I left partway through my kit overhaul to take a leak outside behind one of the buildings. When I got back, a man named Aggar and several other PKK fighters were milling about my belongings.

"What's inside your bags?" Aggar asked. He was PKK Ali's right-hand man. I was taken aback by his question. It could have been an innocent question, but something in Aggar's voice told me something was up.

"Clothes and gear," I answered as vaguely as I could. I was highly suspicious now, and I didn't want to give these men any info except the bare minimum.

"I see," Aggar said. "Any electronics?"

"I have a computer," I replied, and with this answer one of the other PKK started rummaging through my bag. I kicked the pack away from the searching hands and the man scowled.

"Can we see?"

I had little choice. In the army I had always hated impromptu kit inspections, usually conducted by sergeants with an axe to grind, which always spelled trouble. Inevitably, I would be missing some insignificant piece of kit, and then I would take all kinds of shit. But at the end of the day, you were still a soldier under Canadian law and the Queen's Regulations and Orders. Unsurprisingly, nothing could compare with the stress of a PKK kit inspection.

I knelt down and showed Aggar my civvie clothes, gear, computer and even a flare gun and solar panel I had picked up in a local market in Sulaymaniyah.

"Where's your phone?"

There was no point denying I had one. Aggar and several other fighters in PKK Ali's unit had already seen me using it when I fired off a few messages after my arrival. I patted my pocket. Aggar nodded his head, said, "Thank you," and then left the house. Now I knew that something bad was happening. This wasn't normal behaviour.

I started shoving all of my gear and clothes back into my bags and then opened my computer with a sense of urgency. The brief conversation had rocked me, and there was no doubt that Aggar was preparing to confiscate my phone and computer. I began frantically deleting all the porn on the hard drive in case the chaste and celibate PKK should find it. Just as I deleted the last file, one of the PKK fighters entered the room and motioned for me to join him outside. I sighed with relief that I had managed to delete everything and then stashed the computer away.

When I walked into the evening air, PKK Ali was on his cellphone, leaning against a stone wall, with Aggar at his side. The last time I had seen PKK Ali in Sulaymaniyah, he had been all smiles and jovial, and was the same when I first arrived on his base not even an hour earlier. But he didn't look jovial any longer. He dropped the phone slightly from his ear and waved me over, and then pointed to Aggar while resuming his phone conversation. Aggar hadn't seemed overly friendly, and his face seemed more rigid now, as did PKK Ali's, and I knew from their expressions that a lot would change in the next few moments.

"We need your phone and computer," Aggar said, with PKK Ali nodding in agreement. Aggar was polite, but his tone made it clear that this wasn't a request.

"Why?"

"For your safety. These things are distractions." It doesn't matter where you are in the world; when you are getting fucked, it's always for your own good and safety. "Now please get them."

"No."

Now it was Aggar's turn to be taken aback. "No," I repeated, sternly, and put on a calculated show of indignance. I was alone in a strange land with people who had been designated as terrorists, and I knew I wasn't going to win this battle. Still, I had learned on the streets of my youth that a thug only respects force and that a show of strength is always better than a display of weakness. It's the law of the jungle, or in this case, the law of the desert.

Aggar wore a look of creeping anger and turned to PKK Ali, who abruptly ended his call. The two men spoke briefly and PKK Ali shot me a look of surprise and anger when he understood my defiance. Aggar rounded on me, and this time he was menacing. "If you want your safety, you will hand over your computer and phone now!" His raised voice brought a handful of other Kurds to the entrance of the main building and they looked on at the standoff. I saw the onlookers at the door and realized that PKK Ali and Aggar wouldn't be able to back down with the spectators watching. They couldn't afford to lose face in front of their own men, and I figured I had pushed them far enough. The computer

44

I could live without, grudgingly, but I desperately didn't want to give up my phone, my only link to the world outside of PKK Ali's unit. I felt I would be helpless without it and that my chances of eventually leaving these guys would be severely diminished.

"You can have my computer, but I need my phone to talk to my family." There was no way they were having the phone. I offered a way for all of us to get out of this with our egos intact. I ended up keeping the phone, but the fact that I had to fight for that privilege told me I was in bad company.

THINGS DIDN'T GET ANY BETTER AFTER THAT. I HADN'T MADE friends with PKK Ali and Aggar, and now it was time to alienate the ordinary rank and file of the unit.

PKK Ali's fighters, about fifty men and half a dozen women, were dressed in an assortment of olive-green and drab-brown garb, which blends well into the bleak and barren landscape of Kurdistan. The fighters were further outfitted with black-and-white checkered headscarves, bandoliers of ammunition and AK-47s. In broken English, the men and even some of the women fighters started pressing me to wear their style of uniform. They weren't at all happy when I said that I wouldn't, choosing instead to wear the multi-camo uniform that I had brought from Canada. I also had a British army–issued combat coat in an arid camo pattern that would keep me warm in the Kurdish winter weather. I had traded some Canadian Forces gear to an English soldier stationed at CFB Suffield in southern Alberta. (Somewhere out there, a quartermaster with the PPCLI is losing his mind on reading about this unauthorized kit exchange, but it happens between soldiers all the time.) The kit

I had arrived in Kurdistan with was badass, and I wasn't about to exchange it for a PKK guerilla uniform.

The PKK also asked me to assume a nom de guerre. Other Western volunteers who arrived in Iraq and Syria after me have chosen ridiculous names to go into battle with. Some are Kurdish names and others are just stupid, like Necromancer and War Hammer. I can remotely understand assuming a Kurdish name in the hopes of fitting in better, but the people who fall into the second category have watched too many movies. I told my PKK hosts just to call me Dillon. Even though I was with the PKK, I was first and foremost a Canadian volunteer and I had absolutely no desire to assume a false Kurdish identity. I could tell that that ruffled their feathers, and I worried I hadn't made a good first impression. For the first time since embarking on my mission to fight ISIS, I realized I had made a mistake. Lieutenant Ali had been right: I shouldn't have gotten mixed up with these people.

The PKK has always been a nationalist guerrilla movement, but it is also staunchly committed to communism. During any downtime, the PKK fighters would take the opportunity to try to indoctrinate me on matters of state and the theories of militant socialism. The PKK are hardcore Stalinists, and they are driven by a peculiar religious fervency. Their founder, Abdullah Ocalan, who was imprisoned by Turkey for thirty years, is worshipped as a deity, and Marx, Lenin, Mao and Castro are his prophets. As with good communists everywhere, God has no place within their ranks—nor do Mohammed or the Koran, from what I could tell. Suffice to say, ISIS has a special kind of loathing for the secular-atheist PKK.

"What do you think of communism? What do you think of Che Guevara, Chávez and Castro?" the PKK often asked.

"Uh, they are okay, I guess," I would answer, out of self-preservation and nothing more. I really thought, *I hate communism, and your attempts at re-educating me are a pathetic waste of time,* but I was playing the game.

Unfortunately for the true believers in the PKK, their attempts to sway me were a notch below futile. I'm from small-town rural Ontario and a strain of libertarian conservatism runs through my bones. Hell, my own father is a member of provincial Parliament in the Conservative caucus, so it's genetic. Of course, I never told the PKK this bit of information. Listening to them talk in broken English about equality, comradeship, American imperialism and the trials and tribulations facing the workers of the world was a small price to pay for the chance to get at ISIS. Such nonsensical discourse would be a dream for all the university kids back at home enrolled in Marxist-theory courses. You see them proudly wearing shirts and caps emblazoned with Che's iconic image. Those people disgust me with their ignorance, but if it took giving communist tyrants an intellectual pass on mass murder and economic ruin in the remoteness of Iraq to get some trigger time against ISIS, then so be it. Hell, I would have quoted from Mao's *Little Red Book* if it would help me get to the front sooner. I just grinned and bore the nonsense.

At least the PKK weren't hypocrites, though; it was impossible for me to doubt their commitment to the flawed communist ideology. I'll give them that much. You can see it in their quest for equality, that most beloved and sacred tenet of communism.

The PKK and the Syrian branch of the same movement, the YPG, are dedicated to equality, with women serving alongside men in combat roles. This strident gender equality is another thorn in the side of ISIS. That's putting it mildly. Battlefield rape is only the beginning for the women of the PKK and YPG who are captured by the jihadis in combat. If the women are young and attractive, sex slavery comes next. Yet no matter the age or beauty, torture and death are the results. It is common knowledge in Kurdistan that it's better to save a final bullet for yourself than to be captured by the enemy. This wisdom is even truer for the female fighters.

I personally don't agree with women being on the front lines for a variety of reasons, mostly because to me it goes against the laws of nature, but at the same time I saw their effectiveness against the enemy, especially as snipers. The Kurds aren't really in a position to turn away female fighters, because they are outnumbered by ISIS and the stakes that are attached to a Kurdish military defeat are way too high. In traditional European and Western styles of warfare, the custom is to spare women and children. This ethos simply doesn't exist with the jihadis. If Kurdistan were overrun by the ISIS hordes, the women would suffer just as much as the men, maybe even more so, so I suppose they have a right to be on the front.

There was one woman in PKK Ali's unit who was stunningly beautiful, with long, shiny black hair and a fit body that showed even when covered in ugly, ill-fitting and unflattering military attire. She was also remarkably deadly and had accounted for several long-distance kills with a sniper rifle. Her name was Zende, and she caught my eye almost immediately. I looked away only when I remembered Lieutenant Ali's words of caution about staying away from the PKK women. But a woman like that is really hard to ignore.

BESIDES SHUNNING AN ASSUMED PKK IDENTITY AND FEIGNING interest in communism and Marx, I was issued a weapon on my second day with the PKK. I asked for and received an M16, instead of the more commonly found AK-47. Only one other PKK fighter on base had an M16, and he had it equipped with a sick thermal optical scope that turns the darkest night into day. Optics of any kind are extremely rare in Kurdistan. Some of the other weapons I saw included homemade .50-calibre sniper rifles, light machine guns and mortars. However, the most interesting beast of war on base was what I called "the Kill-Dozer," a bulldozer that had been modified for battle. The cab was armoured with metal plates and there were portholes to shoot from. The Kill-Dozer was just one example of how necessity and a lack of resources have forced the Kurds to get creative with their weaponry.

I took part in some training exercises with the fighters, mostly clearing houses while in an advancing manoeuvre. Taking back territory from ISIS can be painfully slow and costly in human life. ISIS is adept at lacing towns, villages and homes with mines and IEDs, and they are often clever and sinister in their placement. They mine doors and entries, as well as bridges and gardens. Sometimes the jihadis will deliberately leave their black-and-white flags hanging in abandoned positions that they have mined the shit out of, tempting Kurdish soldiers who want to claim a battlefield trophy. The Germans in the Second World War did the same thing with Nazi flags.

All this poses a huge challenge for the Kurds, because whenever ISIS is defeated in battle, the Kurds have to waste time by disabling all the mines and homemade explosive devices left behind. This hinders the advance and allows ISIS to make short tactical withdrawals while depriving the Kurds of decisive victories. But to save the lives of soldiers, there is no other option than to slowly and methodically clear houses of the mines and traps. However, the

PKK is primarily a guerilla force, and most of its members' training is ambush-oriented and done deep in the Qandil Mountains.

I tried to pass on some of the training I had learned while in the Canadian army, but the PKK were dismissive. They apparently knew best and didn't care to learn about "corner drills" and Canadian techniques for clearing rooms with the "cutting the pie" technique. They were equally ambivalent about the importance of not telescoping your rifle barrel when firing from windows and concealed positions, in order not to give your position away to the enemy. They didn't care to learn anything new.

The camp routine was fairly predictable. We woke up at 0530 hours, ate a breakfast of beans, rice and bread, did some training until lunch—which was again beans, rice and bread—relaxed in the afternoon and then ate some more beans, rice and bread for dinner. Often I would catch the PKK fighters eyeing my phone, and I never trusted leaving my gear unattended. The PKK live an austere existence, based on a lack of resources, but also in accordance with their communist ideology. It's hard to find a chair or couch in a PKK base because they are considered unnecessary luxuries. My quarters were no different, containing only our weapons and the uncomfortable bedrolls that we slept upon.

One of the fighters I shared the room with was named Mark. His real name was Merxas, but it had been anglicized to Mark when he had lived in London. He could speak a semblance of English and was a nice enough guy; however, Mark had come from a troubled past that included a stint in a British jail for robbery and drug charges.

In between getting caught up with British law, my new roommate had met a girl and was madly in love. The problem was that his now ex-girlfriend didn't feel quite the same way and wouldn't respond to his texts or calls. Mark asked and pleaded with me to message the girl on his behalf with declarations of love and longing, and though it was awkward, I sent the texts. The girl wrote back, basically saying, "Fuck off" and that she didn't care that Mark was risking his life fighting ISIS and might be killed any day. She was a white Brit and the war didn't concern her. Mark repeatedly asked me to keep messaging this chick, but eventually I said no because it had gotten too stupid.

All PKK fighters take a vow of celibacy because they have to be fully devoted to the Kurdish nation and nothing else. However, Mark would have broken this rule in a second for the girl in England. I'm not sure what the PKK protocol is for texting ex-girlfriends, but judging by his discretion, it was probably frowned upon. Not that I cared. I actually felt for the poor lovesick soldier and could relate. I had recently come out of a relationship with a girl back in Canada, and though I missed the idea of being with her, it wasn't meant to be. Her name was Veronica, and I thought about her throughout my mission and sometimes texted her when I had a bit of downtime. Things were never good enough when we were together, and she still had plenty of First World problems to complain about while I was in Iraq. Most civilian problems seem pretty trivial in comparison to being in a war zone, fighting against ISIS, and I would just shake my head and laugh out of frustration when she complained about staying late at work or having to go to a wedding that she really didn't want to be at. Veronica has a place in my heart, but like I said, it wasn't meant to be.

# 4.

# FIRST FIRE

THE PKK BASE WAS CLOSE ENOUGH TO THE FRONT THAT WE could see the enemy lines over a kilometre away. Their flags were visible, but not much else. Through binoculars we could see enemy trucks periodically arrive to resupply the enemy, but there were never any quality targets. Firing at this range would be useless and mostly a waste of ammunition. It was the same for the enemy, but that didn't stop the jihadis from taking potshots at us, hoping to get lucky with a one-in-a-million shot.

I had been warned that the base often came under indirect fire from ISIS fighters, and on the second night, while sitting around drinking tea after dinner, I heard a series of thuds smacking the upper exterior wall of our compound.

"Daesh bullets," Mark said to me, probably seeing the confused look on my face. I was ready to don my gear and assume battle stations, but the rest of the Kurds paid the harassing enemy fire little if any attention. They were used to it and knew that they were safe in the compound. A few of the men went outside and blasted their rifles towards the enemy and then returned a moment later. They were just letting ISIS know that we were still around, that they wouldn't have their way with us if they tried anything.

My blood was up from the enemy fire and the Kurdish response, and though it wasn't a close call by any stretch of the imagination, it was my first whiff of enemy fire and I had a hard time sleeping that night. Yet this was nothing compared to what I was to witness in the coming days. Not even close.

## 23 NOVEMBER 2014

SENTRIES WERE NEEDED TO KEEP WATCH OF THE BASE'S PER-imeter at night, and I volunteered right away. Would I rather have had an extra few hours of sleep? Most definitely. But what was needed now was a calculated show of enthusiasm and eagerness for the PKK. PKK Ali seemed surprised by my keenness, given our earlier showdown over my phone, but nodded approvingly nonetheless when I stepped up for the night's watch. My rehabilitation among the PKK had begun. I didn't need to be friends with them, but I did need to be confident that they wouldn't knife me in the back.

Sentry duty meant keeping to the shadows, watching and waiting quietly for any disturbance and hoping to God that nothing happened. If everything went well you could crawl back onto your thin mat that we called a bed and sleep a few more hours until sunrise.

In Afghanistan, I had pulled sentry duty on a rotational basis at Camp Phoenix, which meant sitting in an RG-31 armoured vehicle, staring at a screen being fed live video streams of the camp's perimeter. The Taliban's weapons of choice included trucks heavily laden with explosives and driven by suicidal jihadis.

On just my second night in Afghanistan, a special-forces base less than a kilometre from Camp Phoenix was rocked by a 2,000-kilogram car bomb and a follow-through suicide attack with small arms. You don't forget being woken up out of bed from a shockwave like that.

The Taliban used suicide bombers to instil terror in their enemies, but these attacks were primarily attritional and psychological in nature. Unfortunately for the Kurds, ISIS picked up where the Taliban left off, vastly improving upon the tactical application of the vehicle-borne suicide attack.

An ISIS attack often starts with simultaneous detonations of suicide vehicles laden with oil and explosives. These suicide trucks blow multiple holes in the Kurdish lines and signal the beginning of a larger attack. ISIS fighters take advantage of the temporary chaos and confusion and funnel into the newly created gaps, threatening the flanks and rear of the Kurdish forces, all too often causing panic and retreat. (At the time of writing, ISIS has taken the city of Ramadi, using similar tactics.)

I LOOKED UP TO THE MOON, PARTIALLY SHROUDED IN CLOUDS, and stamped my feet to keep warm in the desert cold. The front was covered in darkness and seemed quiet, but that meant nothing. ISIS fighters were only a kilometre away, well within range of delivering indirect fire or worse, launching a suicide attack that would blow the exposed outpost apart. If that happened, I would dive into the closest of the unfinished concrete blockhouses and try to survive the initial blast. After that, I would fire my M16 at the enemy, being sure to save one final bullet for myself. Your mind wanders into dark places when you are tired in the night.

There were rumours of the enemy being equipped with night vision goggles, and that's what scared me most of all. One man with a set of night vision goggles would be godlike in this war, and that thought alone caused me to instinctually dip my head lower into the sandbag redoubt. I needed my own NVGs, but the flight to Kurdistan and accompanying preparations had decimated my bank account, leaving meagre savings that were nowhere close enough to affording even a basic set of goggles.

There were a couple of other Kurds standing watch, and the smoke from their cigarettes caught in my nose. The smell of burning tobacco triggered my own addiction and I pulled a dart from my pocket and ducked low in the fortification so that no one in the desert would see the spark of the lighter. I exhaled and looked above the topmost edge of the sandbag wall encompassing my cold body, keeping the red tip of the cigarette out of sight. A military jet buzzed somewhere high above in the night sky, its engine partially masking the other sounds of the desert. There were the calls of strange animals and muffled voices, but whether they were Kurd or Arab, I could not say. I looked at my watch and was happy that my shift was over in thirty minutes. But the hours spent under the winter moon had given me what I needed: time alone to figure out what I should do about my situation.

A big part of me wanted to get as far away from PKK Ali as I could. I didn't trust him or his companions, and they didn't trust me either. The problem was that Lieutenant Ali was far away in Jalula, so there was no chance of him coming to get me.

I toyed with the idea of hiking through the desert to the closest town, but there were too many things that could go wrong, like losing my way, being caught by an ISIS patrol or being fired upon by friendlies in the night. Stealing a truck was a marginally better idea, but it carried the risk of probably being summarily executed by PKK Ali's men if caught. So I resigned myself that there would be no quick fix to my situation. Unlike the heat of battle, this wasn't a time for rashness. It was a time for calculated thought. There would be opportunities to escape; of that I was sure. What those opportunities would look like was unclear, but I would bide my time knowing that they would come.

Now was the time for alertness. There were people outside the FOB and their muffled voices had returned. Were they Kurd or Arab? I let the cigarette drop from my mouth and crushed it with my boot into the dirt. I wondered if the other guards on sentry duty could hear the voices too. They should be able to tell if they were Arabic or Kurdish, friend or foe. I scurried from my post to where the closest Kurd on duty should have been, but the post was vacant. *What the fuck?* I thought to myself. I checked in the concrete house adjacent to the small redoubt. It was barren too. *Can no one else hear these sounds? And where are the other sentries?*

My rifle was loaded and I waited, listening for something, but hearing nothing except my own breathing and pumping heart. *Someone is out there.* I knew it. I could feel it instinctively, like when an animal knows a predator is close by. I wanted to warn PKK Ali and the men, but I couldn't leave my post, especially when the next closest sentry was missing. My small pack was lying at my boots, and I crouched low over it and untied the string to open it up. I carried a small mag light and stuck it in my mouth, pointing its beam into the opened bag. With my hands free I rummaged through the stored items until my fingers felt the flare gun. I couldn't believe I was actually going to use this thing, but I didn't want to start shooting at ambiguous targets in the night for fear of killing one of our own. I loaded the flare and pointed the device into the night sky. *Is this how I'm supposed to do it?* I had never fired a flare gun before and wasn't sure. I pulled the trigger, and the flare rocketed into the darkened sky and then lit up the night. At first I couldn't see anything, except the desolate land-scape and quivering shadows. And then—moving shadows. There were people out there.

The FOB started coming to life after I fired the flare. Apparently, there were other sentries awake after all, and they started calling to one another in their own language. Then the bullets started flying. In the diminished light and at this distance, I couldn't see if the people outside the FOB were ISIS or Kurd, but their rifles answered that question soon enough. Bullets spattered the base, and then the darkness reclaimed the light. PKK fighters began firing into the blackness, but by the time the next set of flares shot into the sky, the enemy had vanished. Nobody was wounded or killed; it was simply a skirmish that the defenders of this out-post had grown accustomed to. PKK Ali found me and gave me a fatherly pat on the shoulder as if to say "well done," and the next day I had my computer back.

# 5.

# A SAVAGE SPECTACLE

24 NOVEMBER 2014
THE ENCOUNTER WITH THE ENEMY WAS MORE OR LESS ROUTINE, and there was hardly any mention of it the next morning at breakfast. I was tired but happy that my rehabilitation after the phone and computer incident was well under way.

A shipment of supplies awaited us: ammunition, guns and recoilless rifles. Maybe other stuff, too, but as usual the PKK figured I didn't need to know too much, even though I was going with the convoy of two trucks to pick it all up and haul it back to our base. Like guerilla forces the world over, the PKK are always in need of military supplies. Sure, they capture some gear from the enemy when the opportunity arises, but they buy and trade much of their hardware in the murky underworld of arms dealing.

The shipment destined for PKK Ali's men was cached somewhere to the east through a Shia-controlled enclave. That much I did know, because at the last minute, a third truck joined our convoy, not because it was needed to transport the gear, but because three trucks travelling together is safer than two and you never can really trust the Shia. "They're Arabs, after all," the Kurds would say.

PKK Ali rode in the first vehicle with a complement of armed men. The middle vehicle was outfitted with a machine gun mounted in the bed, and the third vehicle in the mini-convoy carried the driver, Aggar in the passenger seat, and me, with two of the PKK women, in the back. Zende was squished next to me, but I didn't mind. Of all the fighters to be pressed next to in a backseat on a bumpy road, she was the best. It was way better than being stuck with one of the sweaty and unshowered men. I tried talking to her, but there wasn't a lot we could say to each other. Instead, I listened as she chatted in her own language to the second woman sitting next to her and closed my eyes until we came to a check-point on the road manned by Peshmerga soldiers, who waved us through. From that point on, we travelled parallel to an empty stretch of no-man's-land. A low earthen berm gave the road some shelter, but it wasn't much, and in some places nothing at all.

One lone, sad-looking bunker caught my eye. It was small, made of concrete and nestled into the berm. Some old graffiti was painted on one of its concrete walls, which was the only sign that it had ever been occupied, but whoever had been stationed at this remote posting had already left it. That was probably for the best, because a handful of soldiers guarding this worthless piece of real estate would be sitting ducks for ISIS. There was not much else around, and definitely no support should the bearded jihadis make an appearance—just empty land that, apparently, nobody on either side of the war wanted to occupy.

The convoy stopped, and two men from the second vehicle climbed into the truck bed and manned the heavy gun in case the enemy tried to mess with us on this barren stretch of land. An ambush was possible. So was sniper fire. Periodically, I could see the enemy's distant flags fluttering in the cold air, and we knew that ISIS was out there. We rolled on.

One of the men in the back of the second vehicle started shouting and banging on the roof of the truck with a heavy fist, and the convoy accelerated rapidly. Somewhere there was a hidden ISIS sniper taking potshots at us and we raced on, not bothering to stop and locate the bastard. In moments like this, it's better to run rather than stick around and give the enemy time to adjust their sights and take another round of shots. I never saw or heard the bullets, but the men with the machine gun felt them whistle by and were crouched low to hide from the fire. Luckily, it amounted to nothing more, as we put distance between us and the hidden gunman. That was a good thing, because we had real problems to start worrying about, specifically our passage into the Shia-controlled enclave.

I knew we had arrived because of the different flags flying along the bunkers and checkpoints at the side of the road. The Kurdish flags were gone, and now Iranian banners and green flags signalled Tehran's influence over the Shia fighters. These guys were no friends of the Kurds; allies out of necessity would be far more accurate. There is a mutual distrust based on history and ethnicity. The Kurds are Kurds and the Shia are Arabs. It seems all the same to us in the Western world, but to these guys there is a world of difference. Nevertheless, the common enemy of ISIS keeps them from each other's throats—for now. I have no doubt that when the Caliphate comes tumbling down, the Kurds will have to defend their borders against the same Shia militias that they are currently "allied" with. But that's the way of the Middle East. It's like a great big game of Risk or Diplomacy, with everybody backstabbing and screwing each other over. The only problem is that this is real life and you can't sweep the pieces off the board and walk away. Otherwise, you'll be dead.

The Shia fighters looked a lot like the ISIS jihadis to me. They wore big, thick beards and shambled around with a lack of professional discipline. PKK Ali talked to the armed men guarding the road, attempting to gain a passage, but it looked to me like our trip would go no further.

"What's happening?" I asked Aggar, but he shrugged his shoulders and began to get out of the vehicle. Aggar took three paces towards PKK Ali's lead vehicle and was greeted by the flurry of a dozen rifles cocked, raised and pointed at his face, with another half dozen trained on the rest of us inside the truck. *Son of a bitch!* The Shia's yells and screams and weapons halted Aggar in his tracks. He brought his hands up above his head and hunched his neck as if bracing himself for what would come next. *They're going to fucking waste us.* I had this gut feeling that it would happen. All it would take was one trigger-happy gunman to blow him away, and then the other guns would go off like a string of firecrackers and we would all be dead in our vehicles. *Get back in the fucking truck, Aggar!*

"Whoa, whoa." PKK Ali's voice cut above the din. The words mean the same in Kurdish as they do in English. It's the universal phrase for "everybody chill the fuck out." PKK Ali walked slowly and cautiously between the gunmen and Aggar, who was frozen in place. He then gingerly pushed Aggar backwards to the passenger seat, and I heard him sigh deeply when he was seated and the door closed.

Sweat beaded over my brow and my heart pounded. I could only imagine what Aggar had felt in that moment, but he kept his mouth shut and didn't say anything. It was only when Zende released her grip that I noticed she had my forearm clenched in her hands, and we looked at each other with nervous smiles.

Some of the Shia disappeared, but there was still more than enough left to take us out in an efficient manner. Everybody stayed put, except for PKK Ali, who was on his cellphone, pacing the length of his truck. He was talking to someone, and then, with a cigarette stuck in the corner of his mouth, he dialled a new number. Again, he started talking. Aggar turned his head around and finally said something when he saw me staring at his commander. "He knows people," was all he said.

*I sure as hell hope so!* I would have peeled out of there faster than you can say "infidel," but PKK Ali was a stubborn bastard. There were weapons somewhere on the other side of this checkpoint, and getting our hands on them could mean the difference between life and death in any future battle with ISIS.

"He knows people," Aggar said again and pointed through the windshield. The Shia fighters had cleared off to the side and were lifting the rail blocking the road. I didn't know whether to be happy or afraid as they let us through the gates.


IT WAS A GOOD STASH OF WEAPONRY: AK-47S, DRAGUNOV SNIPER rifles, recoilless rifles and mortars, with plenty of ammunition. All Soviet-made, of course. We carried it all out, piece by piece, box by box, from the warehouse to our waiting vehicles, and I could tell from the looks on everyone's faces that they desperately needed this gear for their fight against ISIS. PKK Ali had the biggest smile of all and patted me on the back, as if our earlier altercation over my phone and computer had never happened.

It had been at least two hours since we passed through the Shia checkpoint, and now we had to make our way back through the same gates. *Hopefully, leaving will be easier than entering*, I thought. Surely it would, because if the Shia were going to kill us, it probably would have happened already.

We rolled through the streets of the town, escorted by two Shia militia vehicles, one in the lead and one in the back so that we were hemmed in and our speed controlled. I could feel our truck begin to slow and match the reduced speed of the vehicles to our front. The speedometer fell and then fell some more until our tires were basically crawling along the road. *What the hell is going on?* It turns out that our escort wanted to show us something before we left the Shia-controlled territory.

Along the side of the road was a ghastly spectacle. There were corpses lying on the side of the road, and it looked like they had been dead for a while. The faces of the deceased were bearded and grotesque in appearance, except for one body that was missing its head entirely. Lieutenant Ali and other Peshmerga fighters had warned me about the Shia lopping off heads, and this looked like evidence to me. The headless man and the others lying on the ground were probably ISIS fighters, but I wasn't sure.

Our convoy lingered for a moment, with the eyes of the dead staring blankly through our windows. Zende grabbed my hand and squeezed it. The older woman was closest to the window and looked away. Aggar and our driver lit cigarettes and stared ahead. Everyone was quiet. Finally, the lead Shia vehicle carried on and we left the enclave under the watchful eyes of the militiamen. Everything about this incident had been planned. The Shia were aping ISIS and sending the Kurds a message by way of complete brutality: "Don't fuck with us or this is what will happen to you." In this part of the world, making a political statement with the use of corpses as props isn't entirely out of the ordinary. Liberal democracy is a long ways off here. I lit a cigarette and drew deeply when the green flags of the Shia were behind us. To me, they look an awful lot like the black-and-white flags of ISIS, and the devil can take them all.

THE DRIVE BACK TO BASE WAS WELCOMINGLY UNEVENTFUL. NO sniper fire. No hassles at checkpoints. We needed it that way, because after a day like this, your mind craves the silent nothingness of a drive through empty land. I think Aggar was still shaken up over having twelve rifles pointed at his face, and all of us were still sickened by the sight of the decapitated heads.

Watching the terrain fly by without incident was good, but even better was that Zende nudged and touched my arm while either pointing stuff out to me along the drive or stressing a point in our severely broken conversation. She was hot, and I'm not just saying that because it had been a while since I had seen many women.

When we got back to base, we unloaded all the weaponry into a shipping container. It was like Christmas for the PKK. That night, we ate beans, rice and bread for dinner, the standard fare on the Kurdish front lines. In accordance with communist austerity, chairs and tables were mostly nonexistent and the fighters typically all sat together to eat as a way to build camaraderie and reinforce the belief in equality.

Lieutenant Ali's final words to me about not touching the women was pretty simple advice, but at the same time, it was utterly difficult to abide by. War and sex go hand in hand—they always have. In fact, I'm convinced that the reason so many people join the army is because of sex. As clichéd as it sounds, women love a man in uniform, and compared to the PKK guerilla attire, my uniform was slick and had Western style. Maybe that's why Zende was interested in me. The fact that I was the lone white guy on the entire front probably had something to do with it as well. Whatever it was, we were catching each other's eye and glimpses, and a part of me thought it was becoming obvious. But the other fighters in the room had their own issues and problems to focus on—everybody does—and so from across the room I let my eyes wander up and down Zende's body as discreetly as I could.

After dinner, the evening routine set in. People drank tea, engulfed in a cloud of blue smoke that billowed from dozens of cigarettes darting out from nearly every mouth. The Kurds love to smoke, and in this cold weather a pot of tea was a minor luxury that we couldn't live without. It kept us warm, and though it wasn't as good as coffee, the caffeine helped keep us alert. I rose from the floor, leaving the men huddled around their hot drinks, and headed for the door. There were times when the PKK would literally keep an eye on me as I urinated or had a bowel movement, such was their apprehension or distrust of me. But this time nobody stirred as I stepped into the night. It was too cold for them to be bothered, and seriously, where could I go and what trouble could I find in the middle of nowhere?

However, I had ulterior motives for leaving the house that didn't include taking a slash or a crap. It was a ploy. I lingered at the doorway just long enough to catch Zende's attention. I held her eyes for a second longer than was necessary and then walked outside. There was no doubt in my mind that she would follow, and when she did, we stole away to one of the empty concrete houses on the base. There would be sentries somewhere, but they paid us no mind and we didn't see them anyway.

Zende led the way and was the first in the door to the empty house. It was the women's quarters, and she knew what she was doing. Guaranteed, she had thought about this as much as I had over the last few days. As soon as we were inside, our hands moved frantically over each other. We both knew there wasn't much time, and half of our uniforms stayed on, while the other articles that were in the way were strewn onto a pile on the cold floor. After the day I had been through and everything else in the past week, I needed to be with a woman. It made things a lot better.

I'm not sure what was more reckless—some of the things I did under fire while in Iraq, or having sex with a woman of the PKK. Clearly, I wasn't thinking with my head, but it had to be done. We kissed before I left the house and I steadied myself as I walked back into the main compound, where the fighters were still smoking and drinking tea. I felt good and scared at the same time. I had been gone for less than ten minutes—not a lot of time for my absence to be noted. But Zende was still gone, and if anyone connected the dots I would be in a world of shit. I might even be killed. I learned later on that anything was possible with these people.

With a freshly poured tea, I stuck a cigarette in my mouth and acted super-chill as I reached for my lighter. *Be cool. Be cool—shit!* My entire body froze when I realized that I had left my coat, with the lighter, back in Zende's quarters. *Damn it!* So much for acting chill.

I finished the tea quickly, thinking the entire time that I was surely going to get caught for what had just happened. Somebody would know, and if they didn't, Zende would talk, like all girls do, and word would get out. Then the wrath of PKK Ali would descend on me like a tonne of cinder blocks. Goddamn it. But it had been worth it.

The next morning, I found my coat neatly folded on a cinder block outside my door.

## 26 NOVEMBER 2014
## PKK BASE

THE MOON WAS STILL HIGH IN THE NIGHT SKY WHEN THE PKK camp came to life. I checked my watch, and it was still too early for the start of our day, but clearly something was up. Everybody was crawling out of sleeping bags and rolling up bedrolls.

"Pack one small bag. We will be gone for a while," Aggar said to me. Mark, the love-stricken fighter with a disinterested girl in England, did the same, as did every other fighter. Truck engines were being fired up outside, and the quiet of night vanished with the approach of battle. There were heavy guns firing in the distance, the explosions thumping dully on my ears. There was a fight somewhere along the front, and though I wasn't told anything, every instinct inside screamed that combat was near. I packed my small camo bag with medical supplies (gauze and bandages), cigarettes, a flashlight, a headlamp, spare ammunition and a canteen that I was in too much of a rush to fill up. It was really cold outside, colder than you would ever imagine Iraq to be, and so I wore gloves and pulled a black toque over my head to cover my ears. I strapped on my tactical vest, clipped on my Kevlar helmet and put four mags in the sleeves of my vest. I grabbed the M16 rifle that was always by my side and then stepped into the night, eyes wide, excited and ready for war, adrenaline pumping furiously.

Fighters were loading their gear into several idling pickup trucks. I saw Zende, with her sniper rifle, hop into the bed of a waiting truck along with a few of the other female fighters. I had been given no further instructions, so I jumped in with them. We saw each other, and I remembered how she looked and felt when we were alone, but there wasn't much time for that. Women are distractions in battle, and a big one was coming fast.

"Dillon!" PKK Ali's voice called out above the din of the truck engines and the fighters prepping for battle. I pretended not to hear.

"Dillon!" This time it was Aggar's voice, and he was moving down the line of trucks, looking for me. He stopped when he saw me with the PKK women. "You ride with me," he said. I unloaded from the truck, grabbed my bag and saw Zende shoot me a subtle look of disappointment in the darkness. At any other time I would have lingered, but this wasn't the right moment. I jumped into the back of PKK Ali's truck. Apparently, the commander wanted to keep me close at hand for the coming battle. Mark followed suit, as did Aggar, and there was another Kurd that I recognized as Brothahan. PKK Ali sat in the front passenger seat with a driver, and we led the convoy over dark roads towards the sounds of the guns.

# 6.

# TAL AL-WARD

**26 NOVEMBER 2014**
**TAL AL-WARD VILLAGE (20 KILOMETRES SOUTH OF KIRKUK)**
**1430 HRS**
FROM THE BACK OF THE TRUCK, I SCOPED THE GROUND THAT LAY ahead and then stripped off one of the black gloves protecting my hands from the desert cold. The wind quickly sapped the warmth from my exposed skin, but my fingers moved quickly, dialling the lens to focus on the chaotic scene of battle ahead.

Through the lens I could see a long earthen berm stretching across the barren landscape, its concrete bunkers and redoubts manned by a mixed force of Kurdish Peshmerga and PKK soldiers numbering in the hundreds, perhaps close to a thousand strong. Even at this distance their small individual figures were recognizable; some were firing from behind the cover of green sandbag fortifications, while most seemed to be milling about the base of the defensive berm, where enemy bullets could not reach.

I tucked the scope safely into a pocket in my combat pack, pulled the black glove back over my hand and looked on as a mobile rocket battery prepared to let loose another salvo of Katyusha rockets. Its crew buzzed about the massive truck with the launcher attached to its bed. When the missiles fired from the stacked tubes, they made a howling, screaming noise that cut through the metallic chatter of small-arms fire at the front. The noise reminded me instantly of newsreel footage from the Second World War, when Red Army rockets and artillery pounded the Germans along the eastern front. Hopefully, ISIS was catching just as much hell as the tattered Wehrmacht had in the dying days of that long-ago war.

*This is it. This is what I came here for,* I thought. The white Toyota pickup truck idled briefly, allowing me and the other armed men a chance to survey the unfolding battle before slowly rolling on. Now we were just twenty metres away from the wall of dirt that separates Kurdistan from the Islamic State. *Soon. Very soon.* I began to instinctively check my gear: the action on my M16 rifle, the straps on my TAC vest, the clips on my helmet— the small kinds of things soldiers do to maximize preparedness and, more important, pretend we have some control over our own destiny when on Ares's chessboard.

The late-afternoon sun was trying to emerge from behind a clouded sky, but its struggling rays did little to take the chill out of the onset of winter. The driver turned the wheel abruptly to bring the truck's course parallel with the length of the Kurdish defensive berm. The white Toyota was indistinguishable from the dozens of other trucks of the same make, model and colour that were parked at random along the front, and the Kurds manning the berm's firing step paid us newcomers little mind, as ISIS was just seventy metres away, entrenched in their own fortified mounds of sand lying along the opposite bank of a slow-moving canal. Across the stagnant north-south waterway was the small village locals called Tal al-Ward, and beyond that, a large hill that dominated the surrounding countryside for miles around. You couldn't miss it.

In a terrain marked by its uniform flatness, the hill was the only physical feature of note and an obvious strategic position. It rose in length for five hundred metres until its ends tapered back to the desert floor, and it was topped with a sunken road that twisted in a concealed fashion along its spine. Mounds of dirt, concrete bunkers and trenches adorned its crest and sheltered the dug-in jihadi defenders. From up high the jihadis held a vantage point from which they could rain bullets down on the Kurds with impunity. A quick look was all it took to tell me that if we were to beat the enemy on this day, we would have to climb and secure the hill's malicious slopes.

A hill of this size doesn't exist naturally in central Iraq. It was created out of necessity and for survival. When ISIS forces spilled out of Syria and blitzed towards Erbil, Baghdad and Kirkuk in June 2014, it set off a frenzy of construction. Bulldozers, backhoes and all varieties of heavy machinery were enlisted to scrape, pile and shape the earth in one nearly continuous line of defensive fortifications that stretch from Iran to what used to be the Syrian border.

A thousand kilometres of opposing trenches stretch all the way across north-central Iraq. It was very much First World War–style warfare. On one side, the Kurdish forces defend their homeland, and on the other the black flags of ISIS fly. A modern-day no-man's-land separates the two forces. In most places, that no-man's-land can be measured in kilometres, but at Tal al-Ward, it could have been done with fifty metres of tape.

The construction crews assigned to dig the hills and trenches learned early the wisdom of bolting thick metal plates over their cabs to save themselves from jihadi snipers. The impromptu construction likely saved Kurdistan from the customary rape and pillage that follow the march of the Caliphate's black-and-white flags. To this day, whenever ground is taken or lost, the heavy machinery is never far behind, ready to build the next series of defensive works that mark the shifting tide of battle and war.

PKK Ali rolled down the window and called out something from the cab of the truck, and immediately, his men began getting ready in earnest. Brothahan knocked on my helmet with a closed fist and used his thumb to make a cutting motion across his neck. When the driver applied the brakes, everyone jumped from the truck bed onto the hard dirt. In the Canadian army there would be orders and a plan, but this was Iraq, and even if there was a strategy, I couldn't understand the language it was spoken in. I hopped from the truck and ran for the base of the four-and-a-half-metre-high earthen berm, M16 firmly in hand. My GoPro camera and battle gear rattled against my body, minus the helmet, which I left behind in the bed of the truck. Bothahan was sending me a message earlier with his throat-cutting hand gesture. If you're an ISIS sniper, who are you going to aim for: the generic Kurd or the white guy decked out in a $500 piece of protective headgear? Ditching the helmet made me less of a target.

I wasted little time in scrambling up to the berm's ledge to get a view of the surroundings. On my left and right, men fired their weapons, mostly Kalashnikovs, at an opposing earthwork that rose from across the canal. ISIS fighters were quick to return the fire. Their bearded faces would bob up to let loose bursts of fire and would then vanish just as quickly into a myriad of foxholes and trenches. The Kurds on my flank fought in the same way, but with clean-shaven faces.

A mere twelve hours previous, the berms, village and hill had been securely in Peshmerga hands, giving them a commanding vantage point from which to spot an ISIS attack from miles around. Yet ISIS now held the high ground and, by extension, the village.

One of the ironies of this war is that ISIS is much better armed and equipped than the "good guys," courtesy of the United States. When the Iraqi army fled before the ISIS advance on Mosul and northern Iraq in June 2014, they left behind two divisions' worth of sophisticated American weaponry. Tanks, armoured vehicles, assault weapons, even attack helicopters fell into the hands of the Islamic State in the summer of 2014. Kurdish arms are antiquated by comparison. The Kurds rely mostly on relics of the Soviet era, giving ISIS the tactical advantage that enabled their forces to sweep across Syria and Iraq in a modern-day blitzkrieg.

The previous night, ISIS had attacked the Kurdish FOB at Tal al-Ward and swept up the commanding hillside. It was rumoured among the Kurds that ISIS fighters carried night vision goggles and, under the cover of darkness, delivered a surprise attack that killed many of their comrades in their trenches and drove the survivors from the position.

That's why we were called in. We had to retake the hill at Tal al-Ward.

## KURDISH DEFENSIVE LINES AT TAL AL-WARD
## 1500 HRS
ROUNDS WERE COMING IN HOT AND THE KURDS TOOK TURNS alternating between ducking their heads and firing their rifles at

the enemy. I had come to Iraq to fight and was happy at the chance to finally get in some trigger time. Once on the firing step, I blasted away at the enemy entrenchments—ineffectual suppression fire, but I had travelled over ten thousand kilometres for this opportunity and it felt good nonetheless. I emptied a clip, fired off another burst from my M16 and then slid back down the berm, taking a seat in a long line of Kurds sitting along the sheltered slope that was completely covered in garbage, mostly plastic bags and discarded water bottles. It was a safe place to be, so long as an ISIS mortar shell didn't plunge from the sky. But you can't hide from that kind of death anyway.

Small-arms fire rattled up and down the line, Katyusha rockets screamed overhead, men sat around smoking cigarettes and chatting, others scurried about with cellphones and rocket-propelled grenades. An attractive black-haired woman just a little older than Zende strolled by with a long sniper rifle braced over her shoulder with one hand.

The small-arms fire would rise and fall at random, but there was always a strange background noise emanating throughout the front. It sounded like a thousand voices were crying out in various emotions.

The ferocity of the small-arms fire rose once more. "They're getting some!" I shouted to a young man my own age sitting just a few feet away. The Kurd wore a closely shaved Mohawk and looked at me with a bewildered expression. That happened quite often.

PKK Ali put a hand on my shoulder and motioned for me to follow him. We hurried along the base of the berm and through the tangled groupings of soldiers until a large, concrete-fortified redoubt blocked our path, marking the entrance to the one bridge that spanned the canal. A small cluster of men waited there, including a cameraman from a Kurdish news agency who wore a wide-brimmed straw hat and a baby-blue dress shirt tucked into his trousers. The sight of the camera held over the man's shoulder reminded me to turn on my own GoPro camera strapped across my chest. I peeked around the edge of the bunker to the opposite bank of the canal, where only moments before a body of about fifty Kurdish fighters had stormed the bridge and made a beachhead. They were clawing their way up the ISIS-held position and into the village while taking heavy fire. Some were wounded, others dead. I could easily hear the rhythmic *thump-thump-thump* of a Soviet-made DShK heavy machine gun, which ISIS had strategically placed atop one of the big hill's bunkers. The DShK is a beast of a weapon that can take down a low-flying helicopter and can easily tear a man in two with rounds the size of a fist. Clumps of dirt spouted from the ground surrounding the breach, marking the ferocity of the incoming enemy rounds.

There was only one way across the canal: a single bridge about fifty metres long that spanned the water. Like the rest of the country, the Kurds were on one side and ISIS was on the other. PKK Ali shoved my shoulder again. There was no common language between us, but his meaning was clear as he gestured to the bridge and the beachhead in front. I looked into the PKK commander's eyes and nodded my head in understanding and then agreement. If we were going to cross, there could be no hesitation. No time to think or question. I had come here to kill the enemy. The enemy was over the bridge, so that's where I had to go.

While the mass of Kurdish soldiers continued firing from their own lines, PKK Ali began sprinting from the cover of the protective berm and then raced for the bridge. I followed as quickly as I could, knowing that if I stopped to think about the madness of our charge, I would be dead. Bullets were snapping all around, hitting the bridge and the water in the canal below. It was a straight dash from one killing zone on the bridge to another on the far bank. I could hear and feel my heart beating, the adrenaline pumping through my muscles as I reached the halfway mark of the bridge and then kept going, fighting hard to keep up with the older Kurd's pace. My legs felt weighted down by stones, but it was all in my head. My body was fit and I pushed myself faster and harder, knowing that every second spent on the bridge increased the odds of taking a piece of lead.

A bullet struck a steel beam, the sound clanging in my ears just as we cleared the final metres of the bridge and then galloped for the breach in the ISIS lines. PKK Ali shouted something incoherent at me before quickly blending into the tip of the Kurdish spear that was now moving into the village. Once ISIS's defensive works were punctured at the bridge, their fighters withdrew from the riverbank and into the village, leaving their dead behind.

In hindsight, ISIS's first defensive berm was relatively lightly defended. I don't think they intended to hold the works along the canal, or the village, for any length of time. Rather, their goal was to conduct a fighting withdrawal, whereby ground was traded for lives. ISIS wanted to weaken the attacking Kurdish force before we reached their main position atop the hill. It was a sound strategy, but the Kurds were willing to oblige in the exchange, even though it meant casualties. But that's the way it is in Iraq.

ONCE INSIDE, THE SOUNDS OF SHOOTING AND YELLING ECHOED off the hovels and down the streets of the village. Every ramshackle house, every window and stone wall, was a potential ambush site. The Kurdish assault force was about fifty strong, minus one man who got hit twice in the arm almost right away. I moved with them through the confusing maze of streets and alleyways that were littered with rubbish. We moved cautiously, other times at a run, until we arrived at a concrete wall that marked the end of the cluster of homes. The large fortified hill now loomed immediately to our front and I could see it being raked by small-arms fire.

A Kurdish fighter poked his head over the village wall, which provoked an instantaneous spray of fire from ISIS fighters. The Kurds responded by sticking their rifles over the wall, firing blindly at the enemy. Most carried Kalashnikovs, but a few of the luckier ones were armed, like me, with Western rifles, either bought in local markets or stripped from enemy corpses. I took my turn and fired a burst over the wall and then stepped back, brushing up against a unit commander who was talking furiously into a cell-phone with a voice raised above the crescendo of rifle fire.

There are not many radios in the Peshmerga, so orders and the progress of battle are relayed to command centres and subordinates through personal electronic devices. The presence of cellphones in combat seemed strange, but even stranger was the reappearance of the Kurdish cameraman, who was diligently capturing the chaos of war for the news. He scurried about, immersed in his work, getting close-up shots of the fighters and paying no attention at all to the pieces of the concrete wall chipping into the air from the incoming rounds.

Suddenly the cry of *"Daesh!"* rang through the air and there was confusion. One of the commanders got a text on his phone that there was an ISIS force hidden in the village and we were about to get ambushed. Some of the PKK even started backtracking from the protective wall. They were afraid of being killed—or worse, captured. PKK Ali sent me off with a half dozen other men and we patrolled about fifty metres through the village, circling houses and climbing over stone walls, making sure the area of operation was clear. We came across the bodies of jihadis, Kurds and civilians. Some had been killed hours before and some more recently.

Yet the perimeter was clear. The thrust of the Kurdish spearhead had seemingly cleared ISIS from the canal and the village. Now it was time to retake the hill. The original force of fifty men had been augmented by a few more reinforcements from across the canal—mostly PKK, though there was a sprinkling of Peshmerga. A rudimentary plan to seize the high ground directly in front was devised under the strain of incoming fire. The commanders talked among themselves and on their phones, and then the orders were given. It wasn't a glamorous plan, the kind the great military minds of history, such as Napoleon or Stonewall Jackson, would be proud of. It was simple, direct and to the point: a frontal charge up the hill. No real tactics involved at all, just brute force and an acceptance of casualties to achieve the objective. Years of war have made life cheap in Iraq. Maybe that's the way it had to be in this brutal land.

It was time for the real fighting and the real killing to begin.

# 7.

# THE GREATEST DAY OF MY LIFE

*Today I bore witness to intense savage combat to retake
a small town. I came through unscathed but the same cannot
be said for all of us including some unlucky daesh.*
—Dillon Hillier, Facebook. 26 November 2014

"UP!"

I rose from the ground, panting and focused. The village was behind me and the enemy to the front. There was only one way to go, and that was forward.

"He sees me. Down!" The command echoed in my mind. I grunted as I once again buried myself into the ground to hide from the enemy fire.

"Up! . . . He sees me. Down! . . . Up! . . . He sees me. Down!" It's a drill every Canadian soldier learns. Infantrymen in the Canadian army know what it means to be lying in an empty field of snow, wheezing air, waiting for a sergeant to bark that first word. "Up!" and the soldier lifts from the ground, weighted down in full battle gear, and begins to sprint. But his legs and arms pump for a mere fraction of a second, certainly not enough time to build any momentum, before the sergeant shouts the second part of the drill. "He sees me. Down!" And on that last word, the soldier drops back to the ground, having covered maybe five metres. The soldier gasps, looks to the end of the field, which seems no closer, and waits for the sergeant to bark the command once more. And so the process continues until your lungs scream for mercy and muscles begin to seize. It's a Cold War–era drill devised to limit a soldier's exposure while simultaneously covering ground in a frontal attack. "Up! . . . He sees me. Down! Up! . . . He sees me. Down!"

"Up!" and I rose once more. Only this time I ignored the second part of the command and maintained the sprint until I was within reach of a small berm. I dove and embraced the shelter. Bullets were snapping the air and raking the hillside from every direction, and I used the lull in my drills to recalibrate my situational awareness. The Kurds had begun moving up the slope, but ISIS was contesting the ground from behind the countless bunkers and trenches that laced the hillside. Their bearded faces would emerge to fire a few shots, and then they would dip back into the labyrinth of fortifications.

A mixed cluster of a half dozen Peshmerga and PKK scrambled to the small berm that I had taken shelter behind, and their rush provoked a flurry of bullets that blew up the surrounding ground. The Kurds hugged the Iraqi earth just like me until the fire abated, and then, like madmen, we gathered our courage and stormed towards the next trench.

The attacking spearhead moved in small groups like this, ducking, hiding and firing as they went. There was no way to avoid casualties in this type of fighting, and men went down dying and clutching ghastly wounds as they charged forward. But the Kurdish progress was undeniable. I increased the tempo of my pace in order to stride over a dead jihadi who lay in my path. His body was a blur of black clothing and reddened skin—evidence that the enemy was taking casualties too.

Suddenly, a group of four bearded men sprouted from a hole in the ground, flushed up from the Kurdish advance like a covey of quail in tall grass. They ran for the top of the hill and the safety of the sunken road at the top. If only they could reach the final berm, they would be safe, at least for a while, and they ran with the fear of death.

This was the first time I took deliberate aim at a man. I brought the M16 rifle to my shoulder and, with the flanking Kurds beside me, fired rapid bursts at the enemy. Blood misted the air, and at least two of the ISIS fighters staggered over the lip of the berm that marked the main enemy works running along the spine of the hill. *Unlucky motherfuckers.*

Scenes like this repeated as the Kurdish drive picked up momentum. Peshmerga and PKK soldiers were streaming across the bridge now and into the village. The battle was reaching its climax and the ISIS fighters prepared as best they could for their last stand. The battle would be won or lost along the berms guarding the sunken road that ran along the length of the hill's spine, and it was this position that ISIS had withdrawn to. Their bunkers swarmed with jihadi fighters, and the heavy DShK machine gun kept thumping away at the easy Kurdish targets attempting to gain the hill.

The sunken road along the top of the hill was concealed from the view of observers below. You couldn't see it from the village or the base of the hill, but it was there and protected by bunkers and a zigzagging berm that paralleled both sides. But the road also swooped down to the base of the hill, and if we could reach it, we would have the opportunity to flank the enemy and start rolling up their position.

The ad hoc section of Kurdish fighters that had formed around me broke cover again and stormed over the berm protecting the lower reaches of the sunken road. Two of the four ISIS fighters we had fired at lay dead on the dirt road, one with his back patterned in a tight grouping of bullet holes. More blood trailed up the road, leading into a concrete bunker and indicating that wounded combatants might be close by. The group approached the structure cautiously, and for the first time I realized that Brothahan was with me. I hardly knew the man, but I was happy that a vaguely familiar face was present.

Brothahan was the one who approached the bunker first. There was no "cutting of the pie," as would be done in the Canadian army, when a soldier slowly and cautiously moves in a pie-shaped fashion across the opening of a room in order to properly work the angles of sight. Instead, Brothahan struck his gun around the bunker's entrance and sprayed its inside. We checked after, but there was no one inside. They got lucky, but then we got lucky next. Right away, bullets started whistling by us. If you can hear the *whoosh*, the bullet is no farther than a couple of metres away. Luckily, no one was hit. We darted behind the bunker's concrete siding and returned the fire. The jihadis withdrew further up the road and we moved on in pursuit like a pack of wolves after a wounded stag.

My ad hoc section darted in short bursts to avoid the enemy fire, which was constant and increased in ferocity the closer we got to the top. It was a running gunfight. We moved, and ISIS would fall back to the next zigzag in the berm. We were firing our weapons relentlessly, more to suppress the enemy than anything else, but a few times jihadists lined up with my sights.

The road and hill were partially enveloped in smoke, which created an eerie feeling as more Kurds piled up the slope and spilled over the protective berm, giving steam and confidence to the attack. But the thumping DShK told that the battle was not over and that ISIS was fighting on. We pressed the attack, past more trenches, bunkers and blue tarps with fifty-gallon water tanks that marked where the enemy had slept the night before. Kurdish flags—the red, white and green tricolour with a yellow sunburst in the middle—fluttered above some of the strongpoints, but that meant nothing. ISIS uses deception; they're good at it, actually. Their fighters will wear Kurdish civilian clothes to get close and will fly Kurdish flags to indicate that areas are safe and under Kurdish control. But these are carefully planned traps meant to lull victims into a false sense of security.

Along the sunken road were abandoned white Toyota pickup trucks, the same type we rode to battle in, parked haphazardly, some with their windows and tires blown out. I looked down and saw another dead ISIS fighter. He was leaning against a flat tire, but I had only a moment to study the body for move-ment before a Kurd aired the corpse out with a burst from his Kalashnikov. You can't take chances in Iraq, and if the jihadi wasn't dead before, he was now. The group paused to take stock of their situation.

In battle, you know only what you can see around you. It was clear to me that, at least in our section of the field, we were winning. There were more enemy bodies on the ground, but at the same time, we knew the fighting was still going strong along the rest of the hill because of the gunfire. My section had grown to maybe twenty men by this point, maturing from an infantry section to a platoon. I felt good. I felt we were winning.

We halted the advance for a breather and to take stock of the fluid situation, while waiting for the commander to make a phone call on his cell. This is when we got in the shit pretty bad. For some reason, there was a large gap in the berm facing west. I can only guess that it was to allow vehicles a quick escape straight down the face of the hill, instead of using the switchbacks.

A number of ISIS fighters appeared through the gap on the reverse slope. They were running from something, and they scared the shit out of us. As soon as they opened fire, I saw Brothahan go down. He was within arm's reach of me and got zipped in the face. Everyone dove for whatever cover we could find and began trading gunfire. It was beyond intense. A few Kurds tried to out-flank the enemy, but they got pinned down by more enemy fire that came from God knows where.

There was blood in the air when Brothahan got hit, and I had assumed he'd been killed outright. That would be the logical assumption when someone is shot in the face. But a moment after lying on the ground motionless, Brothahan began to twitch and then started clutching at his face, which was a mess of blood and bone. It was pathetic and heart-wrenching to see. The Kurds called out to Brothahan through the buzz of bullets whipping overhead, probably telling him to stay still because he was drawing fire to himself. Their voices cried with hopelessness. *This man's going to die on the ground right in front of me.* It was just a matter of time before another enemy bullet struck him. I broke cover and rushed towards the stricken Kurd about a dozen metres away.

I shouldn't have done it. It was reckless—stupid, even. But I wasn't thinking, just reacting. I think it was my training that kicked in. There's an unwritten rule that you don't leave a wounded man behind. My hands reached under his shoulders and started dragging him towards the closest cover I could find.

Together, Brothahan and I made easy targets, and the enemy bullets zeroed in on us. Thankfully, the rest of the Kurds helped by firing their weapons to give as much suppressing fire as they could until the jihadis fled back up the hill.

Brothahan was moaning in pain, and I dropped to the ground with exhaustion. My body heaved and my lungs took deep breaths from the exertion as I rummaged through my combat bag for the meagre stash of medical supplies that I carried with me. A couple of Kurds gathered around the wounded man, not knowing what to do. "Tell him he's going to be okay! Tell him!" I shouted at them, even though I knew they wouldn't understand. The truth was that I was saying the words for my own benefit more than anything else. I needed to convince myself. I pulled out a roll of medical gauze from my bag and, with hands shaking from the pumping adrenaline, began the process of patching up the disgusting wound.

In the Canadian army, every soldier is a medic. It starts in basic military training, when you take a beginner first-aid course, and the training builds with each course completed as you advance through the ranks. In the lead-up to Afghanistan, I underwent extensive combat first-aid training, as did every other soldier on deployment. These individual soldiering skills were necessary in a war that killed over 150 Canadians and seriously wounded thousands more. The simple act of carrying a tourniquet and knowing how to use it saved Canadian lives in Afghanistan. It's different in the Kurdish army. There is essentially no first-aid training, knowledge or equipment.

A couple of Kurds stood by, watching, as I unrolled the gauze. They were probably good soldiers, but utterly useless in first aid. They had no idea what to do.

IF IT'S POSSIBLE TO BE LUCKY AFTER GETTING SHOT IN THE FACE, Brothahan is the example, insomuch as he wasn't immediately killed. The bullet had hit his cheek and exited through the ear, creating a vicious wound. If the bullet's trajectory had been even minutely altered—by a shaking hand, a gust of wind, an exhaled breath—Brothahan would have been killed outright. It makes a man question whether it is luck, God, fate or the random chaos of battle that determines life or death in combat. Of course, there is no answer.

As it stood, the wound still threatened to bleed him out in short order, so I wrapped the gauze around Brothahan's head until his entire face was virtually covered, like you see in pictures of maimed and gassed soldiers from the trenches of the First World War. "It's all I can do for him," I shouted at the two men who had been assigned to look after the wounded man. "Tell him he's going to be okay."

I never saw Brothahan again, but I heard afterwards that he lived.

There wasn't any time to dwell on Brothahan's fate. The fighting was getting heavier, as a second Kurdish force was moving up the opposite flank of the hill, squeezing the ISIS defenders between two pincer movements into a shrinking pocket of resistance at the very centre of the high ground.

My platoon pushed on and came to another opening in the western berm. Given what had happened at the last opening, we approached with caution and saw tire tracks rutted into the dirt, leading down the reverse slope. There was a small berm beside the tracks that was just big enough to offer the illusion of safety. A section of men well placed on this reverse slope would be able to wreak havoc and engage the enemy from behind, so our group split into two wings. While the larger group maintained the advance up the main road, my smaller section ventured into the more exposed open ground of the western slope.

It was a good plan, if only you ignored the risks. Being separated took us into dangerous ground, with a heightened risk of being cut off if the attack failed—or, more likely, mistaken as the enemy and taking friendly fire. There had already been a lot of friendly fire that day due to poor communication systems, and I wasn't confident that it wouldn't happen again. Nevertheless, we continued picking our way carefully down the western slope, crouching low and manoeuvring for cover as best we could. Everyone sensed our exposed position while on this dangerous ground. It was too much for some of the men, and half of the six-man detachment made a decision to go no farther. I could hardly blame them. Venturing behind the enemy force posed inherent risks, let alone trigger-happy Kurds further up the hill who could easily mistake us for the enemy.

Words were exchanged with the other two Kurds who were prepared to keep going, but nothing would move them, so the three of us continued on our own. It felt strange to be moving downhill when, for the past hour, we had been moving up, but the battle had changed and this rear-flanking movement offered the best chance of getting some more kills.

I broke from some meagre cover to get into a better position and realized my mistake right away. Immediately, the earth started spitting up around me from enemy fire. *Fuck!* I dropped to the ground and spotted the enemy: two ISIS fighters about 140 metres away. I was their target and their bullets struck all around my position, some within inches. For the briefest of moments, fear paralyzed my body and mind. I had been shot at before, but that was as part of a massive charge, where to the enemy I would have been just another anonymous target. Here, I was the lone target and it was personal. These two jihadists wanted *my* death. I don't know how long they waited before firing, but they chose their timing correctly and waited until I was at my most exposed and vulnerable, with nothing so much as a divot of earth to hide behind. There was nothing else to do but engage, and thankfully my individual soldiering skills kicked in and I started firing back. It felt like an eternity and a split second all at once, but the exchange was probably no more than twenty seconds.

To my good fortune, the two ISIS fighters were not in a good position either. They were just as exposed as I was. They didn't expect to see Kurdish forces this far down the hill and so close to their rear flank, so my appearance was almost as much of a surprise to them as theirs was to me. Luckily, they didn't have enough time to set up a proper ambush.

I kept firing, feeling the butt of my rifle hammer against my shoulder, hoping for my bullets to make contact before theirs did. It was only a matter of time before someone was killed, and I could feel the odds being dialled up against me as the enemy rounds crept closer. There was no doubt in my mind that my marksmanship was probably superior to the enemy's, but they had two guns against my one. The two-to-one ratio flashed through my mind and didn't add up to good odds. Then, suddenly, fate smiled on me like it never has before and probably never will again.

Perhaps their nerves broke from my fire, or maybe they saw something else that threatened their position. I'll never know for sure why the two ISIS fighters inexplicably rose from the ground. At first, I thought they were going to manoeuvre closer so as to get a better position on me, or set up a cross fire. I knew they might not need to move far for either scenario to come to pass. A few metres in either direction could be enough to provide the right angle to lay down accurate fire, and the thought filled me with a dread that I hadn't felt before. I waited for the inevitable, but then something happened: they turned and ran. Even now, when I replay the image of the two jihadis beginning to flee, I get emotional because I know that I had avoided imminent death.

I stuffed my heart back down my throat and felt a surge of relief well deep within my body, because the jihadis had made a mistake; their nerves had broken first in this high-stakes game of chicken. I saw their mistake and knew that they were already dead. It's like I could see with perfect clarity what would happen. The jihadis' lives ended as I knew they would.

I took deliberate aim at the fighter in the lead and squeezed the trigger, watching as he went down in a heap to the ground. While on the run, the second jihadi turned to fire a wild and ineffective burst from his gun. I remained stoic and calm and lined up the sights on my M16. My finger pulled the trigger again and didn't stop until I saw the second target crumple. Two confirmed dead. They were my kills, and for better or worse, I'll always remember their shattered bodies.

Later, I stood over the two bearded corpses and looked down at them. Mere moments before, they had been alive and trying to kill me, but now they were dead. I allowed myself time to wonder what they had thought before I shot and killed them. Maybe they weren't thinking anything, just reacting to the situation, just like I was. The first jihadi to go down had been hit in the head, and his brain was leaking out of a hole in his skull, which had been torn apart. *Unlucky motherfucker.* (I don't know why, but that was my immediate go-to phrase whenever I saw a dead jihadi.) The second had been pierced through his torso a couple of times. Chechen, Afghan, Arab and African passports are often found among the dead ISIS fighters, but these two corpses were native to the Iraqi land in which they had fallen.

While looking down on the two dead jihadis, I remembered exactly how I had felt when I squeezed the trigger. Should I feel guilty for feeling so good at that very moment? Is there something wrong with me for feeling that this was the best thing that I had ever accomplished? Any answer will sound feeble and glib if spoken by someone who has never had to pull a trigger. But men who have seen combat know the truth: in the mind's shadows, there is something profoundly intoxicating about having the power over life and death.

There are a lot of strange feelings that go through your body and mind after killing in combat. It's so hard to explain. Maybe it's futile to even try, and for good reason. One thing is for sure: you are never again the same person after killing a man. Even if it's a jihadi savage who had it coming. The Peshmerga credited me with two confirmed and four other probable kills at Tal al-Ward. Whether it was two or six doesn't really matter. What matters is that there are a few less ISIS fighters because of my actions, and that's something I'll be proud of and carry forever.

‡‡‡

## 26 NOVEMBER
## EVENING

THE SOVIET DSHK HEAVY MACHINE GUN HAD BEEN SILENCED, and with it the last of the jihadis had either been killed or fled down the Western slope, maintaining a fighting withdrawal that took advantage of the Kurds, who had become careless in thinking the battle was over.

In the rush to secure the hill, the Kurds had left the DShK as it was found, pointing down the eastern slope towards the village of Tal al-Ward and the bridge over the stagnant canal. Wisps of smoke still trailed from its heated barrel, which protruded from a slit in a concrete bunker, and as the light faded, I examined how the lethal ground would have looked to its ISIS handlers.

The gun was perfectly placed. The fighters would have been able to sweep the hillside and the bridge with ease. In more experienced hands, not a man could have crossed over the canal alive. Nevertheless, the Russian-forged weapon had on this day done what it was built for. The DShK can take down a low-flying helicopter, so when its fist-sized rounds hit a soldier, the corpse is often unrecognizable. On this night the streets of Erbil and Sulaymaniyah would sound with the wails of widows and orphans because of this beast of war and the carnage it had unleashed. The Kurdish dead scattered across the field of battle was proof of this. Yet the gun was silent now and would do no more harm until the morrow, when it would be turned around to face the enemy.

The hill was now firmly in Kurdish hands, and in the half-light, men fired their weapons down the Western slope into the next line of fortifications that lay beyond. Coloured sparks blasted from rifle barrels, letting loose tracer rounds that raced across the empty land in search of victims. In the distance, pipelines streamed fire and black smoke. Dusk marched on and flares rocketed into the darkened sky, creating a surreal sight. The wounded had been carried away, their cries of agony heard only behind the lines, and in front, the enemy dead shadowed the ground.

When the twilight surrendered to darkness, the rifle fire slowed and then virtually ceased. Aside from the odd rattle, the hill had gone quiet as the Kurds entrenched in the recaptured lines. There would be no surprise ISIS attack like on the previous night. They had been mauled badly and were patching their wounds seven hundred metres away in the same trenches they had started from the night before.

As the Kurds dug in under the winter moon, enjoying tea and sweets left behind by the enemy, coalition air strikes began rocking the jihadist fallback positions in fierce explosions that shook the earth. The bombs turned night into day and I felt the force of each blast pulsate through my body. There were too many air strikes to count. ISIS was in the open, getting pounded, and it was mesmerizing to see and hear.

Sentries and small patrols kept watch of the front, prepared for a counterattack, but ISIS was done. I had survived the battle, saved a man's life and killed the enemy.

When the coalition planes finished their work for the night, we slept in the tents of our enemies. Somewhere a wild dog howled at the moon and the field of battle was left to the dead. That was the battle of Tal al-Ward.

# 8.

# THE WORST DAY OF MY LIFE

**27 NOVEMBER 2014**

THE SLEEP OF THE VICTORIOUS WAS SPORADIC AND RESTLESS.
The tents and makeshift sleeping quarters atop the hill at Tal al-Ward had changed hands twice in the last twenty-four hours, and the brutal struggle for the high ground was seen everywhere. Blood stained the dirt berms and trenches, and countless spent rifle cartridges rolled under combat boots and glinted dully in the morning sun. There was trash everywhere—mainly empty water bottles and open latrines that stank like sewage drains.

The night before, the Kurds had rifled through the enemy bags and packs left behind in search of food, but there was nothing except candy and sweets, which caused terrible pain on empty stomachs. The day's fighting had left me famished, but above all, I craved water. Yet there was none to be found—perhaps not surprising, since I was in a desert. I remembered my own basic training in the Canadian army, where your canteen had to be so full that it could literally not hold one more drop of water, or

95

else some sergeant would take a giant shit on you. I should have heeded that advice, but I had been too excited about the prospect of battle to worry about a canteen. One thing there was an abundance of was canned soft drinks, but I would have traded a flat of Coke for just one mouthful of water in a heartbeat. Yet the Kurds were boiling tea, so there had to be water *somewhere*, and I couldn't understand why they would waste it on a hot drink when our throats were so parched.

And the beds, if you could call them that, atop the hill were thin mats unrolled on the hard ground. ISIS fighters had laid their long, greasy black hair and beards on the same beds the night before, and the thought would have disgusted me if I hadn't been too tired to care. The mats were probably crawling with lice and bedbugs, but that was a problem that seemed small and unimportant after battle.

At some point during the night, ISIS launched a small counterattack, but it was feeble and far enough away from my post to be of little concern. It was most likely a diversion of some kind, or a show of force to keep the Kurds at bay. Still, it woke me from an already restless sleep. So too did the coalition planes roaring overhead, as pilots delivered bombs that detonated less than a kilometre away.

The battle at Tal al-Ward had left ISIS as a paper tiger in this sector, and I yearned for a fresh push against the enemy. But the Kurds were tired from battle and sentry duty. I had taken my turn keeping watch atop the berm, but the land to my front was quiet, or so it seemed. There was not one pair of night or thermal vision goggles on the entire front, which was dangerous because the enemy had them. That's how ISIS had managed the surprise attack that drove the Kurds from Tal al-Ward in the first place. One soldier able to see in the dark is a powerful weapon, and I strained my eyes into the night, worried with the thought that I was being watched. But nothing happened and, when it was my turn, I tried to sleep with what little darkness was left.

## 27 NOVEMBER 2014
## 0700 HRS

MORNING BROUGHT MORE EXHAUSTION AND THIRST AND HUNGER. The berm was stirring to life and I rolled from my mat and cleared the sleep from my eyes. There was nothing to eat, only more candy, and water seemed just as nonexistent as the night before, so I drank a can of soda instead. PKK Ali's soldiers started putting their battle gear back on and prepping their weapons, ready for what the new day might bring. The women in the twenty-man unit did the same, one equipped with a homemade .50-calibre sniper rifle, the others with standard Kalashnikovs. I left the tent and kicked at the empty water bottles strewn on the ground with my boots, looking for a stray bottle that might have some water remaining. There was one, mostly empty and with the cap missing, but it contained enough drops to wet my parched mouth and throat. It was the best I could do.

Word had spread about yesterday's casualties, and PKK Ali called the soldiers together to relay the news. Retaking Tal al-Ward had come at a cost of thirty Kurds killed in combat, with many more wounded—some seriously, like Brothahan. There was no way to be certain how many ISIS fighters had been killed or wounded. Some would have been carried back to their secondary lines, while others still lay on the field. In a war where corpses were often left to putrefy in the desert sun or be torn apart by wild

dogs, comrades on both sides made efforts to bring the dead back
to safety for proper burials.

Yet undoubtedly there were bodies left behind—in fact, some
could be seen from the safety of the hill—so a patrol was needed
to get a rough count of the enemy dead, and PKK Ali would be
leading it.

The unit would move over ground deemed secured, but the
intersecting berms, trenches and gullies at the base of the hill could
easily hide enemy fighters left over from the night before. The
twenty soldiers under PKK Ali's command would move down the
western slope of the hill and sweep the front before re-entering Tal
al-Ward on the reverse slope. Essentially, we were going to circle
the hill. If everything went well, we would be able to get a count
on the enemy KIA and maybe gather some intelligence or find a
wounded prisoner.

Our force left the tents atop the berm and moved in a linear
formation, single file down the western slope into the labyrinth of
trenches and berms. ISIS was less than a kilometre away, so we kept
our heads down and moved cautiously, aware that enemy snipers
would love to get revenge for the previous day's defeat. I heard the
odd crack of solitary rifles, but ISIS seemed just as happy to leave
the patrol alone, so long as we stayed at a safe distance. After all,
they had been mauled at Tal al-Ward by the Kurds and then punished badly by the night's air strikes. I looked at the black flags flying in the distance and wanted to make a push to rout the enemy.
Now wasn't the time to let them catch their breath. We needed
maximum aggression, despite fatigue and hunger, to annihilate
the weakened enemy—that's the Western style of warfare—but
both sides were too tired to do anything more than conduct low-
intensity skirmishing.

So the patrol moved on carefully and the men allowed their rifle barrels to lower, sensing the exhaustion on both sides of the Iraqi no-man's-land. Suddenly, PKK Ali clenched his fist and it rose sharply, and the patrol stopped. There was something out of place up ahead—a body—but was it alive or dead? I took up a covering-fire position as two men moved closer to the human lump resting on the arid floor behind a small mound of dirt. The two Kurds shouldered their rifles and then began dragging the black-clad fighter to the protective safety of a nearby berm.

At first, I thought that perhaps the combatant was still alive, but the thought vanished as the Kurds carelessly released their hold of the corpse and let it flop unceremoniously to the ground. The jihadist's weapon had already been stripped and a pilfering of his pockets revealed that they had already been emptied, or maybe there had been nothing of value to begin with. The man's face was heavily bearded, but his skin looked white, especially in comparison to the tanned Kurds who had manhandled the corpse. More rummaging revealed a tattered and ragged passport, the only thing of significance on his body. The Kurds flipped through the pages of the official documentation and discovered the man's Chechen nationality.

The Chechen fighters in Iraq and Syria have a reputation. They are regarded as the toughest foreign recruits found in the ranks of ISIS. They know how to fight.

It's no surprise, given the history of their country. In the early 1990s, Chechnya was one of many former Soviet satellite states to declare independence. Unfortunately for them, the new Russia wasn't about to give up its North Caucasus holdings without a fight. The first Russian army units to enter the Chechen capital of Grozny were torn apart in urban warfare and sustained up to eighty per cent casualties. The city was largely destroyed, but the Chechens secured their independence for two years. But Chechen independence was a vodka-induced illusion. The Russian bear was merely catching its breath, and two years later its conscript army lumbered into the North Caucasus for a second time. Chechen fighters were driven from the major cities and fled to the mountains, where they began a decades-long guerilla campaign. It was in these mountain redoubts that the Chechen struggle for independence morphed into an Islamic call to jihad. Militants from the Arab world flocked to Chechnya to help repulse the Russian invader, and now the Chechens were returning the favour to their Islamic brethren in the Caliphate.

The Kurds pocketed the passport and moved on.

Despite the lack of valuables on the dead Chechen, I let my mind wander to a faint hope that the next body would yield something more than a passport. I'm a big fan of Bernard Cornwell's *Sharpe* series. In one book, a lowly British soldier loots the corpse of an Indian king and pockets enough jewels and rubies to make him rich for life. Of course that wasn't going to happen at Tal al-Ward, but I would have been happy picking up a weapon that could be resold at a local market, or even better, some cash, or maybe a gold ring or necklaces.

The patrol came across ten corpses at the base of the hill, but there was nothing of value on them except a few more foreign passports from Africa and one rifle. It wasn't clear whether the ISIS corpses had been cleared of their valuables by their own comrades or by the Kurds. Middle Eastern warfare is a lot like the American Wild West. Weapons and loot are claimed from the enemy dead by the man who made the kill, or the first one on the scene. Given the incentive, the bodies found by PKK Ali's patrol could easily have been scavenged by Kurdish soldiers during the night, leaving me empty-handed. If I were with the Canadian army, the dead would not have been looted. But the rules of war in Iraq were different from those that had been enforced by the Canadian Forces in Afghanistan.

The dead jihadis were essentially the same, dressed in a mixture of black garb and Kurdish civilian clothing. Their hair was long, black and greasy, just like their beards, and all were seemingly in their early to mid-thirties. These weren't the indoctrinated child soldiers you read about, but rather men of a prime fighting age in terms of strength and fitness. There was something unusual about them. Each had a red ribbon tied around his arm, like a band. I found out later that these red armbands indicated that these fighters belonged to what ISIS considers an elite unit. They would have received better training and been in possession of better weapons. Perhaps this explains why they were able to initially overrun the Kurdish positions at Tal al-Ward.

Each body was pulled to some form of cover to be dealt with later, and then the patrol began circling to the eastern side of the hill, into the village. The sun was shining and the previous day's cold a thing of the past. There was still no water, though, and I hoped desperately that the village would yield something to quench my thirst and hunger. The cluster of huts and walled narrow streets was exactly as I remembered: cramped and littered with garbage. The fighting had scared most of the locals off, creating an atmosphere of unnatural silence for an urban setting. We searched backyards, wells, gardens, fences and walls, but nothing was found. Then I heard a commotion ahead. My GoPro camera was turned off to conserve battery life, but I turned the chest-mounted device back on and started recording. I rounded the street corner in time to see members of the patrol pointing their rifles at a man who had appeared in the doorway of a home.

The man's arms were up and he waved a greeting to the Kurds, but I could tell from the body language of the patrol members that this wasn't a friendly encounter. "Looks like we're taking a prisoner," I said into the camera. The man went to take a step from the doorway, and as soon as his body moved, the Kurds unleashed a torrent of gunfire that exposed his insides to the air. He fell in a heap to the ground, blood pouring from the multiple holes in his body. I was speechless, shocked by the killing, and I fumbled frantically to turn my camera off. If PKK Ali's men knew I had recorded the killing, a world of trouble would have descended upon me. The red light on the camera was a giveaway. I scrambled with shaking hands to turn it off.

It amounted to murder, as far as I was concerned. There had been no warning shot. They could have even shot him once in the leg, but they literally blew him away instead.

The patrol didn't waste time, moving on with haste and leaving the corpse behind. PKK Ali and Aggar hadn't been the ones to fire, and it looked like they were angry with the actions of their men. I kept up with the fast-moving Kurds, who wanted to put distance between themselves and the scene of the crime, but I stole a last look behind my shoulder. The man's wife and several children emerged from the same doorway and beheld their dead husband and father. A part of me wishes I hadn't taken that last look. I wake up many nights hearing the screams of the man's children and wife, and whenever I think about it, I have to fight back tears. The cries of those kids were sounds so terrible that you don't want to imagine them. It's the worst thing I have ever seen or heard.

It didn't take long for the Kurds to begin making excuses

and justifications for the killing, mostly for the benefit of their Canadian companion. When the patrol cleared the village and we started making our way up the hill, word started spreading that the man was an Arab, not a Kurd, as if that gave them licence for the deed. Mimicking an explosion, the men gestured as if to say he could have been wearing a suicide vest. I didn't buy it, but it was better to go along with the unconvincing claim. PKK Ali and his men didn't want the rest of the Kurdish force to know about what had happened, and if I was suspected of leaking the event or talking to someone in the Peshmerga, it would spell trouble for me.

I tried to push the thought from my mind and carry on with the mission, but it was impossible to forget the casualness of taking what was likely an innocent life. It wasn't a cold-blooded murder, but rather an instinctual response to the slightest possibility of danger. I couldn't comprehend it. But I wasn't in Canada; this was Iraq, and the rules of war didn't exist in this land. This is what happens when civilization retreats: men become animals and the slightest provocation demands a deadly response.

I FELT QUIET REMORSE AS THE PATROL REACHED THE BERM. Flats of water bottles were stacked in the back of a truck, providing me with a needed distraction. I grabbed two bottles and drank greedily, then popped some Tylenol to help with the headache that had been induced by dehydration. I snagged a few more plastic bottles for my pack and then filled my canteen to the brim—my sergeant in basic training would have approved. The platoon used the downtime to eat stale bread and then got some rest in the tents. We would be leaving Tal al-Ward later that afternoon, but there was one more task to take care of.

The Kurdish dead from the previous day had been transported back to Camp K1, but the enemy dead were still strewn on the ground. In this war, when a corpse is exposed to the dangers of enemy fire, it can rot for weeks, months even, until its bones are picked clean by dogs and vultures.

But the jihadi dead at Tal al-Ward were far enough away from ISIS to be properly disposed of, and I volunteered for the job. I wanted to get away from PKK Ali and his men; I hadn't trusted them before and I certainly didn't trust them now, after the murder. There was no enthusiasm among the Kurds for the job. They wanted rest and would have been happy to let the jihadis rot in the sun, but I sighed with relief when selected for burial detail. I stalked off quickly, rifle shouldered, relishing the distance that each step took me from the platoon. I wanted to get away from them, not just now, but forever. I wondered how I might do so as I continued towards the burial site.

Twenty dead ISIS fighters lined the ground, and nearby a bulldozer started, its engine coughing out a black plume of diesel smoke into the air. The heavy machine's tracks rolled over the desert, and then the operator tilted the bucket to make the first scrape into the ground. It took him mere minutes to cut out a suitable trench from the earth, as long as it took for me to smoke two cigarettes as I watched. The bulldozer backed off and we dragged the first dead jihadi to the lip of the trench and dumped him unceremoniously in. The dead move in weird ways, and the corpse's limbs flopped around loosely and in countless unnatural motions. His greasy hair mixed with the dried-out earth. It wasn't a glamorous end, but at the very least the jihadi would be under the earth within the window of time prescribed by Islamic law. It was a lot more than many of the fallen in Iraq receive.

I worked with a half dozen other Kurds as we flung more corpses, one at a time, into the mass grave. Aggar lit a cigarette and then began retrieving another limp jihadi by the shoulders. This one wore black and had a piece of his skull missing. I stared and recognized the dead man as one of my own kills from the previous day. Aggar paused, letting me grab hold of the man's ankles, and together we hefted him into the pit of death. The jihadi stank of shit and urine and I watched without pity as he tumbled into his final resting place, his crumpled head and body landing on the earth. If there were seventy-two virgins waiting for him in heaven, then I would have to account to God for the killing, but if there is an afterlife, surely this man would find a place in hell where he would account for the crimes and atrocities of the Islamic State.

The dead had already been searched and pillaged several times since their last breaths, so there was no point in doing anything else but dumping the bodies. The other ISIS dead, all of them bearded and scraggly looking, were deposited into the same pit, and then the bulldozer's engine coughed back to life. The big blade went to work, scraping and pushing the dirt back and forth until the corpses were covered by a rough mound of sand and earth. The operator drove over the impromptu grave slowly one last time, letting the weight of the machine compress the earth, and then killed the engine. The job was done; the bodies were gone forever and soon forgotten. I wondered at how many unmarked graves could be found in this country; too many to count. Perhaps, like in Flanders and northern France, farmers in Kurdistan will one day find the bones of old fighters popping up in their fields and they will look at them as relics from a past age of gruesome violence. Maybe one day, but I doubt it. Just like I doubted that the mass grave at my feet would be remembered, though I hoped it would.

Not for any moral or sacred reasons, but for sanitation purposes. The village was nearby and if ever peace returned to Tal al-Ward, the locals would need to know where not to dig a well, or build a school, or let their kids play. But this was Iraq, and the idea of a school being built in a land where death and survival supersede all else is laughable.

THE BURIAL DETAIL LEFT THE BURIED CORPSES BEHIND AND returned to the top of the berm. More white pickup trucks were coming and leaving Tal al-Ward, bringing fresh troops to the front and relieving those who had been through hell. More important, they carried water and food supplies, and I helped myself to some bread and a plastic bottle of water. PKK Ali's soldiers had stacked their belongings in a pile and were waiting patiently along the sunken road, some smoking, others resting their eyes. My suspicion of them was growing, and I hastily found my pack in the pile and shouldered it, along with my rifle. I trusted Lieutenant Ali and the Peshmerga to respect my belongings, but not these men. For all I knew they had rifled my belongings while I was burying the dead—not that they would find anything useful. My computer would be a real prize, and it had been left back at the base, unguarded, which made me uneasy. Yet there was no point worrying about it now, as something was happening.

PKK Ali was lounging in the seat of a nearby pickup truck, talking on his phone in a carefree tone. He poked his head out from the window, called out something in Kurdish to his men and then made a circular motion with his index finger. The platoon started gathering their kit, and moments later a front-end loader rolled up to their position, ready to taxi the men off the berm to the canal, where trucks were waiting to convoy them back to Camp K1. I hopped into the dirty bucket with two other men and braced myself for the jostling trip down the berm. I turned my GoPro camera on to get some final footage of the aftermath of battle and captured the tents made out of blue tarps, satellite dishes, fifty-gallon water barrels, white trucks—some with their tires and windows blown out—and a stream of new soldiers arriving to take up their rotation at the front. I panned the camera to take it all in as we rolled away slowly.

The Kurd next to me started shouting and waving his hands in the air. "No! No! No!" is what he was probably saying. I shot him a look as if to say, "Fuck you, I can video what I want," which agitated the man even more. *Fuck these people*, I thought while finishing the pan. I turned the camera off and settled back into the bucket, thankful to be leaving the village, thankful to be heading back to base and hopeful that I could get away from PKK Ali's platoon.

# 9.

# ESCAPE

I WAS HAPPY TO PUT TAL AL-WARD AND ITS NARROW STREETS full of litter and trash behind me. I could say the same about the earthen hill and the stagnant canal and the mass grave full of rotting jihadi corpses. It wasn't out of a sense of remorse over the men I had killed and buried. The fact was that I was still riding an adrenaline high from my first two kills, and the thought that the buried corpses would no longer be cogs in the Caliphate's quest to rape and pillage the landscape filled me with a sense of accomplishment.

Nor was the desire to leave Tal al-Ward founded on regret or shame from seeing an innocent man killed, although I could feel that event beginning to slowly pierce my heart and soul like a cold, steel dagger.

It wasn't my fault. I didn't pull the trigger. Those words were true, yet even though the killing happened too fast for any possible intervention, I was there nonetheless. I was part of PKK Ali's platoon, and because of their animalistic instinct to shoot first and not ask any questions later, I carried a guilty feeling in my heart that wouldn't go away. I recognized the same feeling from a dark night in Afghanistan a year ago, and I fought like hell to bury and forget it by switching my mind to the thought of a proper meal back at base. At Camp K1 there would be more than candy and chocolate bars, and the thought of real food after a forty-eight-hour battle-induced fast was almost enough to drive the thought of the dead Arab or Kurd from my mind. Coke, booze and fucking would work to mask the mental anguish, too, and so would killing more jihadis. Yet another round of battle would no doubt bring about fresh horrors—it always does—meaning that still more combat would be needed to drown the memories gnawing on my soul. It's complicated and messed up, but I felt psychologically trapped in a loop that demanded killing as repentance for previous atrocities. There's no way to get around it: seeing death and killing messes you up.

This psychological trap set in my mind was only half of my current ensnarement. The other half was immediate and visible. After the murder, I knew I had to get away from the PKK. I had joined PKK Ali's platoon because they had offered me an accelerated track into combat against the enemy. That's why I had come to Iraq, and now that I had been in combat, I was anxious to separate myself from the amateurs and rejoin Lieutenant Ali and the Peshmerga. It was a colossal understatement to say the final straw was witnessing the poor civilian bastard getting aired out with a dozen bullet holes through his torso.

Before the trucks departed from the front, I sent Lieutenant Ali a text on Whatsapp, telling him I would be back at Camp K1 within a few hours. One of the Kurds, the same man who had glared at me for using my GoPro camera, squinted at the phone in my hand. I tried to ignore the ill look in the man's beady eyes and then took a final glance at the ISIS lines through my scope and saw that the black flags of the Caliphate had popped up above the enemy fortifications, as if to say, "Here we are. We're not beaten yet. Come at us if you dare." I would have been happy to oblige and come back to Tal al-Ward, so long as it was with Lieutenant Ali and the Peshmerga, rather than PKK Ali and his sketchy band of PKK.

I rested my head on my small pack in the bed of the white Toyota pickup and then closed my eyes. The small convoy rumbled on through the desert, past empty land and small villages, some of which had fallen to ISIS that summer, but which had been recently retaken by the Kurds. Not unlike Tal al-Ward.

The trucks moved as quickly as they could on the decrepit roads towards Camp K1, on the outskirts of Kirkuk, about twenty kilometres away. Kirkuk had avoided the fate of Tal al-Ward and Mosul and hundreds of other villages and towns that fell to ISIS, but it was a close-run thing. Kurds and Arabs both lay claim to the ancient city of nearly a million souls, yet when the shit hit the fan and ISIS blitzed out of their Syrian strongholds, it was the Kurdish Peshmerga that stepped up to defend the city. As at Mosul, the Iraqi army had simply run away, and so the city is held by the Kurds, who have no intention of giving it up, either to ISIS or to the central Iraqi government. No doubt, the possession of Kirkuk will be a battle fought another day.

The presence of Camp K1 immediately adjacent to the northwest of Kirkuk, and the thousands of Peshmerga and PKK soldiers garrisoned within its concrete walls, guarantees the city's safety. It's a massive installation three kilometres wide, consisting of barracks, warehouses and guard towers surrounded by high concrete walls.

When we rolled up to K1 I thought I was looking at a prison rather than a military base. Maybe K1 had been akin to a prison when it garrisoned elements of the Iraqi army. In either event, it was the Peshmerga and PKK who now trained, slept and ate within its walls.

The convoy of trucks approached the main gates of K1 and were waved through the first checkpoint. Armed soldiers watched from a series of checkpoints and towers as the trucks slowly navigated the zigzagging track that led into the sprawling base. I checked my phone for a message from Lieutenant Ali, but there was still nothing. *Where the hell are you, man?*

Once inside, the trucks pulled up to a large building, and PKK Ali's men began unloading their gear and weapons. There were two PKK teenagers standing on sentry duty at the building's entrance, their clothes well pressed and clean, with pistols harnessed in shoulder holsters. They gave me a quizzical look as I walked past them, but they said nothing.

In the front lobby, the smell of food wafted through the air and gave excitement to the men whose stomachs were ravaged with hunger. The pleasant aroma guided the platoon to a banquet hall dominated by a single large table adorned with trays of flatbread, rice and beans, and chicken. A beer would go nicely with the meal, I thought, but that wasn't possible among the present company. There's no sex, drugs, alcohol or fun for the PKK, who live a lifestyle inspired by Stalinist austerity. In their ranks there is no room for vice, except war, and no sin save murder. Still, the food was a welcome relief, and I felt strength and energy return to my body. It was the best meal I had had since arriving in country and I chewed and savoured every morsel, while ignoring the continued stares of the PKK soldiers who were beholding a Canadian for the first time. Most were young, in their teenage years, the sons of high-ranking PKK officials who had nice weaponry and uniforms but were too young to be stationed at the front.

PKK Ali began licking chicken grease and rice off his fingers. The he wiped his hands on his trousers and stood up at the head of the table. It was time for a few words from the commander to his men and women. I'm not sure what he said, but it was a speech containing equal measures of solemnity, laughter and bravado, judging by his tone and the platoon's reaction. They had been through battle, inflicted casualties on the enemy and lost only one of their men. "Brothahan lost his eye but will live." Aggar leaned over to translate PKK Ali's words. Still, it was mostly a time for celebration and happiness. I nodded to Aggar at the news, happy to have done what I could to help the man. A few other soldiers spoke briefly too, followed by a high-ranking PKK official who entered the room for a moment, patting Ali on the shoulder and whispering something into his ear.

The plates and trays were mostly cleared, and I sensed dinner coming to an end. I had compulsively checked my phone since leaving Tal al-Ward, waiting for some word from Lieutenant Ali, but once again there was nothing. Probably two-thirds of the soldiers at K1 were Peshmerga, but that didn't mean I could simply walk up to a new outfit and leave PKK Ali behind. I was a stranger to everyone, there was nobody I could talk to, no one to explain my predicament to, and even if I could find an English speaker, who would care? I couldn't stay on the base by myself without Lieutenant Ali, so I was stuck with the PKK. At least for the time being.

"We're leaving now," Aggar said, and I felt the opportunity to link up with Lieutenant Ali begin slipping by as the fighters began rising from their seats.

"Where are we going?" I asked, but Aggar's response meant nothing to me. He might as well have said the platoon was relocating to Shangri-La.

THINK OF CAMP K1 AS BEING THE HUB ON A BICYCLE WHEEL. THE thousands of soldiers garrisoned within its concrete walls are deployed along a series of spokes to dozens of smaller outposts along the front, basically forward operating bases (FOBs). They are typically walled with concrete or sandbags and house anywhere from a few dozen to a few hundred Kurdish soldiers. Some of the FOBs are well known and situated either directly on the front lines or slightly behind the trenches, creating localized strongpoints. Others are remote and far enough behind the lines to be at no risk of attack because they hold no strategic value.

Despite the Kurds' pleas for more, Western nations provide them with just enough military hardware to hold off the Islamic State's advance, but not enough to enable and supply a large-scale offensive. A few dozen modern tanks with properly trained crews could cut through the Islamic State lines in northern Iraq like a saw through balsa wood, but under the West's austere policy, this will never happen. Not surprisingly, the only tanks found at K1 are obsolete Soviet models.

Yet K1's parkade isn't entirely void of the West's military largesse. There are dozens of lightly armoured vehicles of Western origin, and though they have no real offensive capabilities, the armoured personnel carriers (APCs) provide a method of transportation that protects against enemy sniper and small-arms fire.

I watched as three Peshmerga soldiers climbed into one of the parked APCs and started leading the convoy from K1's twisting exit through arid land towards an unknown FOB. The white Toyotas carrying the PKK followed suit. Before we left, I grabbed my belongings that had been stored on base and was surprised that everything was still there, including my computer. It was a small comfort, but it didn't do much to assuage my distrust of the men I was with. I still had no clear idea of where we were going, but a quick look at the sun's position in the sky indicated a southeasterly direction of travel. The district was called Daquq—that much I knew from studying maps of the region—but beyond that basic fact of geography, I was in the dark. The front was hot here, that much was clear by the presence of checkpoints and more trucks laden with armed men that shared the narrow roads. A burnt-out village with bullet-riddled houses and partially covered ISIS graffiti was further evidence of the ISIS gains that had been rolled back by the Kurds in the last few weeks and months.

My phone vibrated to life in my pocket and I pulled it out eagerly, forgetting the abandoned village now behind us. A white blinking light indicated a new text, and I willed the message to be from Lieutenant Ali. I let out a quiet sigh of relief as I began reading the text. It was short and brief. Lieutenant Ali had been held up but was on his way to K1.

"We already left K1," I tapped out in response, pissed off at Ali for missing the rendezvous, but at the same time happy to have finally re-established contact. "We are somewhere in Daquq," I added.

"When you stop, tell me where you are and we will pick you up."

I pocketed the phone and was finally able to relax, at least a little bit. Another half hour of driving brought the convoy to the perimeter of an FOB consisting of a double line of partially completed blockhouses, concrete barriers and the ever-present walls of sandbags that filled in the gaps. The garrison numbered about 150, half Peshmerga, the other half PKK. The FOB itself was approximately 500 metres by 300, bigger than could be adequately defended with the men available if it came under a serious ISIS attack. The Peshmerga were stationed along the northern half of the FOB's defences, while the PKK held responsibility for the southern defences.

The convoy stopped in a parkade outside the FOB's wire and protective sandbags, and the Kurds began to disembark. The FOB was better than tents in the desert, although it wasn't the greatest accommodation. It was basically a cluster of partially constructed homes in the middle of nowhere, surrounded by a berm and low wall. Before the war, this outpost had been a new settlement under construction. But then ISIS came, and the construction stopped and the would-be inhabitants fled for their lives.

"Where are you?" Lieutenant Ali texted, but I still didn't know. All I could do was give a description of the area, but it was too vague to be of any use. "I'll find out and let you know."

The men unloaded their belongings and headed for a row of uncompleted dwellings. The female fighters found their own house and I took up quarters in one of the better-built houses. The Kurds lined their mats and sleeping bags on bare concrete slabs with personal belongings stacked in no particular order. I found an empty corner and splayed my gear on the hard floor, but I was immediately crowded in by two other fighters who did the same.

THERE'S A FINE LINE BETWEEN BEING A PRISONER AND A GUEST who cannot leave. My place on that continuum wasn't quite clear, but regardless, it wasn't good. Battle and killing had cemented my place in PKK Ali's unit. They trusted me and didn't bother watching me as closely as they had before. Still, it wasn't as though I could leave the base, nor was I free to move about it.

Having a Western-trained veteran in his ranks gave PKK Ali cachet among the other PKK units and a valuable chip in terms of the increased military capacity that I brought to the unit. As far as PKK Ali was concerned, I knew how to shoot, manoeuvre the ground in combat, kill the enemy and patch up wounded fighters like Brothahan. He wasn't about to let me walk away, which meant I was essentially a prisoner without shackles. Yet if I played the game, everyone would pretend that I was just another member of the unit. It was a fraud, of course, but at least the charade would keep me safe from being knifed in the back or taken for a ride into the desert and sold to ISIS (I hoped).

In the meantime, my only recourse was to bide my time and plan an exit strategy that would get me back to Lieutenant Ali and the Peshmerga.


## 30 NOVEMBER 2014
## DAQUQ FRONT

NOT MANY WESTERNERS FLY INTO KURDISTAN'S SULAYMANIYAH airport. Even fewer Canadians make the trip. So it was a massive coincidence that within a few days of my own arrival, another Canadian touched down on the same tarmac, just as the Daquq district 150 kilometres to the west was erupting in battle. Tal al-Ward and several other points along the front had seen fierce clashes between the Caliphate and Kurdish soldiers.

Julien Frechette wasn't a stranger to Kurdistan; he'd been here a few years earlier as part of a film crew documenting refugees. Now he was back with Radio-Canada's all-news network, RDI, reporting on the refugee and military situation in northern Iraq. His first stop was Erbil, capital of the Kurdistan Region, to meet with PKK fighters. The next stop was a small town called Makhmour, followed by a harrowing ride to Kirkuk via pickup truck. "They drive like crazy. No rules of roads," Julien said of the Kurdish drivers. "But if you go to cover a war, you have to go where the fighting is."

For a filmmaker reporting on the war against ISIS, Kirkuk was a city rich in material, given the presence of Camp K1 and its proximity to the front lines. Julien's first few days were relatively quiet and safe, even though you get the feeling in Kurdistan that shit is never too far away. People who have been to Kurdistan can attest to that, and as he departed Kirkuk for an unnamed Kurdish outpost off the highway between Daquq and Kirkuk on the front lines, the veracity of this gut feeling became clear.

The outpost's mixed garrison of PKK fighters and Peshmerga seemed like a logical point for Julien to capture some footage and conduct interviews with the fighters. It was a day of celebration, a Kurdish holiday or commemorative day, and spirits among the Kurds were high, with dancing and singing, and the food was better than usual. The PKK told me that a Western film crew was coming to shoot some footage for a documentary, and I determined to make myself scarce. The PKK is deemed a terrorist group by many countries, due to their decades-long guerilla campaign against Turkey in order to secure a Kurdish homeland. It's complicated geopolitics, and the last thing I wanted was for my face to be associated with a terrorist group. From reading the online comments on a CBC story about my role at Tal al-Ward, I knew that there were a lot of people back home who didn't agree with my mission and who would love to discredit me by saying I was with a terrorist group. As the trucks carrying the filmmakers rolled up to the outpost, I went inside my quarters and closed the door.

I was lying on my bed trying to get some sleep when the door to my room opened. You would think that I would be happy to see another white man in this part of the world, but I was pissed at the sight of him. *How did this reporter find me?* I thought to myself. The PKK was supposed to keep him away, and I had no intention of being on film or interviewed. I looked at the reporter with anger and he looked at me with surprise. "Hello, my name is Julien," he said in a thick French-Canadian accent.

Julien never expected to see a Westerner—much less a Canadian—at the front and initially thought I was a member of Joint Task Force 2 or some other special-forces soldier. I was uncomfortable with his presence and reluctant to talk and so I didn't say too much when I first saw him, but later that night I opened up and discussed my mission.

The PKK had told Julien I was a Canadian army helicopter pilot. I laughed at the suggestion. The PKK had created this ruse and fake identity for me because they knew that I didn't want to be caught on video with an organization that held a place on Western terrorist lists. However, I had made up my mind to tell Julien the truth about who I was and what I was doing. Maybe I was homesick and just wanted to speak to someone in English. It's funny that in Canada, we would have nothing in common, but when situated in a remote FOB on the front lines of the war in Iraq, we practically felt like longtime acquaintances. In any event, I put the PKK's lie about me being a pilot to bed and told Julien I was an Afghanistan veteran on a personal mission to fight against ISIS, and then referred him to Stewart Bell's exposé that had been printed in the *National Post* shortly after my arrival in country. We shot the shit for a while, smoked cigarettes and talked about the war before we both headed off for bed.

THERE WAS AN UNMANNED DRONE FLYING IN THE NIGHT SKY, and ISIS was trying to shoot it down. The Kurds had no problem sleeping through the noise of war. It was normal for them, but not for Julien. He crawled out of bed and stepped outside to take a leak. Immediately, he was under fire.

"The bullets sounded like '*whoosh whoosh whoosh*.' I was being shot at and jumped back inside the house. It was intense," Julien said.

Some of the Kurds woke up but didn't seem at all concerned with Julien's close call. The problem for Julien was that he still had to pee but didn't want to risk his life. Eventually, it came down to a choice between wetting the bed and going for it. A decision had to be made. He went outside again, found some cover to hide behind and finished as quickly as he could before running back inside the concrete house.

I talked to Julien the next day about his close call and told him that taking fire at night was normal and that if he could hear the sounds of the bullets passing, it meant they were probably no more than two metres away. The ISIS main lines were almost a kilometre away from the outpost, and it was possible that the bullets that almost hit him were indirect, long-range fire. Or, the enemy had approached the outpost under darkness and was a lot closer than we thought and was taking deliberate aim. It's impossible to say, but he's lucky to be alive.

Julien left the outpost later that day to shoot some more video at the recent battlefield of Tal al-Ward. He crossed over the same bridge I had run across a few days before. There were still enemy snipers in the area, and so his party was told to cross the bridge in a single row, keeping a distance of three metres between the man in front and the man behind.

"I went across the bridge mellow at first, but then as you reach the halfway mark, you feel the need to get off the bridge as quickly as possible and then you start running."

Even though ISIS was gone from Tal al-Ward, the Kurdish front lines still bore the marks of battle. A large spill from a destroyed pipeline had created a lake of oil that was a mirror reflection of the sky. Julien got some footage and then returned to the outpost, and I agreed to a sit-down interview. He positioned the camera so that it captured the Peshmerga half of the base in the background, rather than the PKK half. At one point I looked away from Julien and turned to speak directly into the camera. I had a special message for my family. I said that I loved them and that if I was killed, it was in doing what I thought was right.

JULIEN LEFT THE FOB, AND I DIDN'T KNOW IT YET, BUT I WOULD be leaving soon as well. We were having lunch the next day when my phone rang. It was Lieutenant Ali. Aggar, PKK Ali and most of the platoon were in the same room and were listening intently when I answered the phone. Lieutenant Ali asked me how I was and if everything was okay. The room had gone silent and all eyes were on me. "Everything is okay, things are fine." I kept my answers very brief and unnaturally stiff. For the Kurds in PKK Ali's unit, my words would have been taken at face value only, but Lieutenant Ali detected something strange in my tone, as I hoped he would. His years working alongside American soldiers had given him an ear for nuances and tone.

"I'm coming to get you. Pass the phone to the commander," Lieutenant Ali said, and I handed the phone to PKK Ali, whose voice raised after a moment as his face turned red. The call ended and he passed the phone back to me without saying anything, though I could tell he was pissed. Would Ali be coming to get me or not? I had no idea what would happen next. But a few hours later a single truck approached the FOB, and four Peshmerga officers got out. They were heavily armed with rifles and sidearms and weren't in a friendly mood. I spotted Lieutenant Ali, and a smile broke across my face. I went to my quarters and started packing up my gear in short order.

I found Lieutenant Ali and PKK Ali in one of the houses, having what sounded like a polite discussion, but the Peshmerga officers holding their rifles at the ready told me that the shit was not very far away. Lieutenant Ali turned to me and said, "Let's go." I nodded my head in goodbye to PKK Ali and then followed the officers to the truck. *Thank God*, I thought to myself. There had been no daring escape, no hike through the desert, no stealing a truck. I had been rescued and let the sense of relief fill my body on the drive back to Sulaymaniyah. Adios, PKK Ali and your murderous band of thugs.

# 10.

# HOME FRONT

THE BIGGEST OBSTACLE TO JOINING THE FIGHT AGAINST ISIS was not the risk of death, or the fear of being captured by the enemy. It wasn't the possibility of being detained by the authorities, nor was it the huge financial and logistical cost. The biggest obstacle by far was knowing the immense strain that my decision had placed upon my family. I struggled with the knowledge that my decision to fight ISIS would bring severe emotional pain to the people I loved most. And it did. This is the soldier's burden. Everyone in my family took it hard, especially my mom, who was a wreck. My parents had a hard time when I was in Afghanistan, but my mission against ISIS was ten times harder on them for obvious reasons. So much could go wrong, and the rest of the Canadian army wouldn't be there to help me out. I was on my own in a strange land, with a brutal enemy nearby.

Everyone in my family was stressed, but they all dealt with the situation in different ways. I'm sorry for the pain that I put my mom through. She cried a lot and had terrible dreams where she could hear me calling out for help. Her way of coping was to avoid all news of ISIS on TV and online, because she was afraid of what she would see. My dad was the exact opposite. For him, knowledge is power, and he read as much as possible about ISIS and quickly became more of an expert on Middle Eastern affairs than the talking heads on TV.

At first, my mission was a secret shared only between family and very close friends. My family wanted to keep it that way, not out of embarrassment, but for my own personal safety. They didn't want me to become a bigger target for the enemy. Yet when my mission hit the front page of the *National Post*, there was no point trying to cover it up. It was in the open. As more media picked up the story, friends and long-lost acquaintances reached out to me, offering their thoughts, prayers and support. That meant a lot.

Besides the mental suffering and worry, my family also had to deal with a multitude of death threats from ISIS sympathizers in Canada. The jihadis sent emails, tweets, Facebook notes and handwritten letters and even called on the phone to threaten the lives of my family members. The RCMP and police were involved in making sure that these threats and the people behind them were managed, and I know at least one guy was taken into custody.

There's a saying that when the police are just minutes away, seconds count. You feel this in a very real way when you open a letter that says everyone in your family will be killed. Needless to say, most of my family slept with adequate protection very close at hand.

My older brother Russell knew more about my plans and mission than anyone else, and he told me that having a family member in a war zone changes you. All of a sudden you gain a new perspective on what's important and what isn't. He stopped paying attention to hockey, politics and sports. He stopped watching TV because those things didn't matter to him anymore. Instead, he scanned the media for stories on ISIS and the Peshmerga, trying to gain a better understanding of what I had gotten myself into. From his perspective, it didn't look good. ISIS was on the move against the Iraqis, the Kurds were launching counterattacks and there was lots of fighting going on everywhere. He saw their sadistic execution methods and knew that a similar fate would await me if I was captured. I know that he also started going to church regularly and often prayed that God would look over me and see me home safely.

But Russell also channelled his worry about my safety into a positive energy that helped me out in ways that I never imagined. I messaged Russell about being in combat at Tal al-Ward. There was some back-and-forth conversation and I told him about crossing the bridge and getting two of the enemy, but there is only so much you can say over text messaging. Finally, he wrote to me and asked what he could do to help.

"Do everything possible to get me night vision goggles," was my response.

That's what he did. As I mentioned before, it's likely that ISIS had had night vision goggles at Tal al-Ward, and I desperately wanted a set of my own to even the odds. Russell took it upon himself to make sure that happened. The only problem was that night vision goggles are expensive, especially the third-generation type I wanted. If he emptied his bank account he could scrape enough money together to buy a set. There would be nothing left over to pay his mortgage or buy groceries, however.

My brother needed at least $8,000, maybe more, to make this happen. That was the minimum amount required to acquire and transport the night vision goggles. A friend and former colleague of Russell's, named Paul Hamnett, working out of member of Parliament Rob Anders's office, recommended that he connect with an elusive Calgary billionaire who had a history of supporting like-minded causes. I won't give his name, but Russell made contact through an intermediary (billionaires don't talk to normal people like us) and their discussion seemed promising at first. I thought to myself, *Holy shit, this guy is going to fund this purchase.* But then things fell through. I'm not sure why, but the message Russell eventually got was essentially "We support your brother, just not financially." Russell knew from his time working in politics that if you don't support a cause financially, you don't actually support the cause. I never once felt like I was entitled or that the billionaire owed me anything, but we were both disappointed. The rejection forced Russell to change tack.

Another friend suggested to Russell that he crowdfund the money. My brother had only a vague understanding of what crowdfunding was, and I had no idea how it worked, either, but Russell looked into it. He put together a short intro message explaining the fundraising campaign, and Paul Hamnett got to work on editing a video that I recorded on my phone and sent from Kurdistan. When everything was complete, Russell clicked on the final button that would make the campaign go live, then donated some of his own money. I never expected what happened next.

By the end of the second day, the campaign had reached $4,000. The crowdfunding site got a lot of attention, and Russell was hammered with requests to go on TV and radio to talk about my mission. CBC News, nationally syndicated talk radio and even small local stations were calling to set up interviews. For a week straight, Russell would leave his classroom at lunch and run to his car to do interviews and drum up support. With every interview, more cash was raised. The day before his Christmas break started, Russell appeared on Ezra Levant's Sun News Network show to promote the crowdfunding campaign, and the ensuing wave of financial support brought in double the amount of money that we had initially asked for. All told, Canadians pitched in close to $20,000.

I thought I knew what it meant to be a proud Canadian before this moment, but I didn't. For me, it is not about watching Team Canada win a gold medal in hockey or fireworks above Parliament Hill on July 1. Being a proud Canadian is about knowing my countrymen had my back when I needed them.

Christmas had come early for me. The money allowed me to buy not just night vision goggles but also armour plating and medical supplies. I carried these with me into battle, and the gear made me a better and more effective soldier. The hundreds of people who helped my mission made a difference, and their generosity isn't forgotten. When I left Kurdistan, I gave the gear to a Kurdish soldier whom I know and trust. He's probably one of the best-equipped soldiers on the front lines, and the gear had been put to good use. When I got back to Canada, I donated the leftover money from the crowdfunding campaign to the families of Corporal Nathan Cirillo and Warrant Officer Patrice Vincent, who were killed in the Canadian terrorist attacks.

# II.

# QUESTIONS AND ANSWERS

IT WAS WITH MIXED FEELINGS THAT I LEFT THE FRONT. TO SAY
I was glad to leave the PKK would be an understatement, but
at the same time I wanted to remain where the fighting was.
I hadn't emptied my bank account to fly halfway around the
world to sit around pretending to be a soldier. I had come to
fight, but that wasn't in the cards for the time being. Lieutenant
Ali and the other officers needed to get back to the Peshmerga
base at Sulaymaniyah, so we drove in a northerly direction. I
caught some sleep in the back of the truck, and when I woke
up, the landscape had begun to change for the better. The drab
brown colouring of the semi-desert region of Kirkuk was gradually shifting to a green hue the closer we got to Sulaymaniyah,
and rolling hills began folding up from the flatlands. It looked
like the kind of land where a civilized people could live and
build a nation, unlike Iraq's middle and southern regions, which
are desolate and barren. With little water, bad soil and no trees, an
outsider would see this land as hardly worth fighting over. And

yet this is a region that has seen fighting and warfare for most of my life.

The roads were good, and at 180 kilometres an hour we completed our drive to Sulaymaniyah in a couple of hours. When you are in a vehicle, 180 kilometres an hour isn't just a number, it's a harrowing expression of recklessness, and your life flashes before your eyes as fast as the landmarks and signs at the side of the road. I wasn't scared too many times while in Iraq, but driving at this speed was an exception. There was nothing to slow us down besides police checkpoints, which were surprisingly well established and reminded me of the customs offices when crossing the Canadian–American border. We arrived at the sprawling Peshmerga military base outside of Suli where my mission had begun about ten days earlier, only now I could better appreciate the size of the base. It was bigger than Kirkuk's K1, with more compounds, soldiers and military vehicles, mostly Russian-made BMP troop carriers, but the odd American-made state-of-the-art MRAP (mine-resistant ambush protected) armoured vehicle was also present, but in smaller numbers. MRAPs were born into the Rhodesian bush war of the 1970s and are built to withstand mine and IED blasts. America deployed over ten thousand of these vehicles to Iraq and Afghanistan during the last decade, but the ones in Sulaymaniyah belonged to the elite Kurdish counterterrorism unit, which was responsible for accumulating a staggering number of ISIS kills.

Though the coming and going of the Kurdish MRAPs hinted at fighting far to the south and west, my time in Sulaymaniyah was marked mostly by idleness. For a week it felt like I did nothing but eat and catch up on sleep. I used this time to contact friends and family to let them know I was safe and go for runs to keep at least a minimal standard of fitness. Though I shouldered an M16 rifle, the Peshmerga were equipped with a variety of different weapons I was unfamiliar with, so I began acquainting myself with the common AK-47, PKC belt-fed machine gun and RPGs. The situation wasn't ideal, but I made the most of my time and at least I was away from the PKK.

In the Canadian army I was a corporal, but with the Peshmerga I was treated as an officer. That meant improved living standards and access to simple luxuries that the rank-and-file Kurdish soldier had to forgo while on duty. Lieutenant Ali had the nicest and largest quarters that I saw while on base, and that's where I slept. I had my own shitty metal-frame bed and enough room for my kit. Other officers of higher rank would often stay there too.

"How did you get the best room on base?" I asked Ali one day.

He laughed. "I create problems for people and then fix them, so a lot of people owe me favours."

Being treated like an officer also meant eating in the officers' mess, which was a cavernous room with a large table and a tile floor. Usually the meals consisted of some variety of rice and beans. There was a functioning kitchen, and even what amounted to a proper shower. The rank and file had to make do with a rusty pipe protruding from a wall, but Lieutenant Ali had plumbers come in to outfit our stall with a proper shower head. I had spent too much time as a grunt in the Canadian army to feel bad about enjoying the luxuries that come with being an officer.

At night I would join Lieutenant Ali and the others in driving into Sulaymaniyah for dinner at local markets, usually kabobs and street meat. I was a guest, and the Kurdish laws of hospitality stated that my money was no good in the company of the Peshmerga officers. It was the same deal if we went to a shisha café. "No,

Dillon. You can't pay," they would say. When I offered to pull sentry duty at night, I was told that it wasn't necessary, because a guest could not be expected to perform such a duty. Not surprisingly, I was okay with that, though a part of me wanted to contribute more than I was. Most of all, I wanted to be back in the fight, where I could see the enemy and make a difference in the world.

Aside from trying to keep fit, eating, sleeping and training with new weapons, I spent a lot of time on my computer and phone. Tinder was a huge distraction for me. Yes, that's right: Tinder. I was shocked and pleasantly surprised that the dating app actually worked in Kurdistan. Unfortunately, it's not as popular in this part of the world as it is in Canada. Kurdish women don't use Tinder, only Western women, and as you can imagine there aren't that many in country. I'll be honest and admit that I swiped right on every profile that appeared, which was probably only four or five at the most. I got a match from a girl originally from Regina who was teaching in Erbil. We texted back and forth, and I found out that she had a reporter friend who wanted to interview me. Next thing I knew, Campbell MacDiarmid from the *National Post* was on his way to Sulaymaniyah from Erbil.

During and since my mission to fight against the Islamic State, I've fulfilled countless media requests, from local Canadian papers to CNN. I like talking about my mission and the things I've seen and done, but I absolutely suck at it. I look back to an interview I did with CTV's Robert Fife shortly after I arrived in Canada and I just shake my head and laugh. Fife and the CTV news crew drove all the way to my parents' house about an hour from Ottawa to do an interview with me. Unless I have a couple drinks in me, I have a hell of a time being at all descriptive. Fife would ask me a really well-thought-out question about a particular incident, like what it feels like to be shot at, and I would just say something like "Yeah, it wasn't really a big deal."

The first journalist I talked to when my mission began was Stew Bell, also with the *National Post*. We talked at length before and after I arrived in Kurdistan, and when I landed in country, the *National Post* printed a lengthy spread about my personal fight against ISIS. It was an amazing piece and I know it made my family and friends proud to read about me in a national paper. Even the Kurds who were included in some of the pictures were ecstatic that they had appeared in a Canadian newspaper, even though they had no idea where Canada was on the map. Still, that story made me slightly uncomfortable because I hadn't actually done anything useful at that point. I had simply landed in country and hung out on a Peshmerga military base.

Yet it was different talking to Campbell MacDiarmid, because by then I had actually done something and been through battle. I was still on a massive high from that action.

"There's a reporter with a Canadian newspaper coming from Erbil. He wants to do a story on me," I said to Lieutenant Ali. Ali didn't need any convincing that this was a good idea.

"Do it," he said excitedly. Lieutenant Ali is a switched-on warrior and a hell of a guy. He always had my back. He's also a shameless self-promoter (he's a great friend so I can say that about him) and so the thought of appearing in a Western paper was a dream for him. Together we went to a Sulaymaniyah hookah bar, fired up the coal in our pipe and waited for MacDiarmid amid a cloud of apple-flavoured smoke. I'm not one to praise foreign cultures, especially for the sake of seeming sophisticated and worldly, but credit is due to the people of the Middle East in their use of the hookah pipe. It's a relaxing way to unwind when you have a few hours to kill.

It was very clear when MacDiarmid arrived. When a white guy with curly hair and a red beard befitting a man with such a Scottish sounding name entered the bar, I rose from my chair and waved him over. Though he wrote for a Canadian paper, Campbell's accent gave him away as a Kiwi. How a New Zealander came to cover the war in Iraq for a Canadian paper is a mystery to me, but here we both were. He is a couple years older than I am and a super-chill dude. Before Iraq, he covered the revolution in Egypt, and as I am writing this book he is still in Kurdistan.

We had a great discussion about my mission, why I was there and what I had done. The Kurds have a completely different concept of personal space than we do, and so Lieutenant Ali had his arm draped over my shoulder while he interjected freely. Once Lieutenant Ali opened his mouth and began talking, you couldn't shut him up. The interview shifted to the battle at Tal al-Ward and again Ali did what he could to make his presence felt. It was during this interview that I learned from Lieutenant Ali that Tal al-Ward had been like a retreat or resort town for "Chemical" Ali, one of Saddam Hussein's henchmen and a first cousin to the former dictator. If you see a picture of the two men side by side, you can easily see the familial resemblance. The thought of Tal al-Ward being anything other than a shithole, let alone a resort, strained all senses of credulity. But then again, this was Iraq.

Chemical Ali was actually born Ali Hassan al-Majid but earned the "Chemical" moniker through his use of mustard gas, sarin and VX poison gas against Kurdish civilians in the late 1980s. In one such attack, over five thousand Kurds were killed. Justice is rare in the Middle East, but Chemical Ali was given his due and hung in 2010 for his crimes against humanity.

Although Lieutenant Ali wasn't present at Tal al-Ward, he was able to fill in some of the gaps in my knowledge, especially in terms of the terrain and overall strategic position of the armies. Campbell took notes furiously, trying to keep pace with the information and anecdotes we were feeding him. He seemed genuinely happy to be doing his job as a reporter. And how could he not? He's a young guy who gets paid to travel to war zones and talk to soldiers for a living. It doesn't get much more epic than that.

"Did you kill anyone at Tal al-Ward?" Of course Campbell had to ask the question. I've also been asked since about the men I've killed and I'm not offended by it in the least. It is an honest question and if you have read this far, you already know that the answer was yes. I'm comfortable talking about killing ISIS fighters now, but at the time of the interview with Campbell, I was unsure what the possible ramifications would be back in Canada. I was pretty sure that I wouldn't be prosecuted for killing ISIS jihadis, but there was still a sliver of doubt in my mind. My father knew I would at some point be asked this question by the media and he advised me to be, at the very least, ambiguous in my answer. I took his words to heart.

"I don't want to talk about that specifically," I said to Campbell. My answer was sufficiently vague, but you didn't have to read between the lines too closely to understand what I was really saying. Whenever a soldier is asked if he has killed anyone and he answers that he doesn't want to talk about it, it means "Yes, I have." I deflected and talked about giving combat first aid to Brothahan, which likely saved his life.

At the end of the interview, we invited Campbell to come back with us to the Pershmerga base and then to the front lines.

"I don't think my editors will allow that and besides, I have no body armour," he said.

"We'll get you some." I have no doubt that Ali could have easily gotten his hands on some, but Campbell never came to the front with us. I think he wanted to, but it just never happened. The interview was published in the *National Post* and once again, a flood of old friends and acquaintances emailed, texted and messaged me with their prayers and thoughts. You can't imagine how much those messages meant to me. As a bonus, Lieutenant Ali got his name in the paper, which he was super stoked about.

I'm not sure how many news stories were printed about my mission, but when I had downtime I would often fire up my computer and read what was being said about me back home. Obviously I had a lot of support from my family and friends, but I was not without my critics. There were a lot of pointy-heads in academia, the military brass and the Canadian government who loved pouring cold water over what I was doing. The common line parroted by these people was that the best way to fight ISIS is through the Canadian army. It's a disingenuous statement at best, but I'll just go ahead and call it a lie. No one in the Canadian military, except for a limited number of special-forces personnel, will ever see the black flags of ISIS, let alone engage in battle against the barbaric jihadis.

Some of the worst criticism levelled by my critics in the media was that I would be helping al-Qaida–affiliated terrorist organizations. Comments like that were low blows that I ignored. Fortunately, I enjoyed a lot of support from current soldiers and recent veterans of the Afghanistan campaign who had seen and knew combat. These are warriors who know the dangers of Islamic jihad and have directly made a difference.

What the journalists and reporters wrote was one thing, but what I really cared about was whether everyday Canadians had my back. The comments sections on the CBC stories were for the most part atrocious. I was called every name in the book, and you didn't have to dig very deep to realize that many of my own countrymen would be happy to see me killed or taken prisoner by the enemy. The cultural relativism is bizarre, and some people's moral compasses are so skewed and twisted that they cannot ever justify military action, even when it's against an enemy like the Islamic State. The great irony is that the left-wing activists who were among those most opposed to my mission would be the first ones thrown off rooftops and beheaded if ISIS ever took over.

But for every negative comment attached to a story on the CBC website, there was a positive comment under stories in the *National Post* and the Sun chain of papers. I'm convinced that despite the vocal criticism from the extreme political left, most Canadians supported my mission, and this knowledge was a huge boost to my morale.

# 12.

# REINFORCEMENTS ARRIVE

## 5 DECEMBER 2014

WHEN I LEFT CANADA, I HARBOURED THE HOPE THAT I WOULD BE the first of several Westerners who would arrive in Kurdistan to fight ISIS in Lieutenant Ali's unit. But by this time, I was still the lone volunteer. The other members of Kerry Dragon's closed Facebook group were no closer to arriving. I told them about being in battle at Tal al-Ward, yet it was becoming apparent that they probably would not be coming. One of the guys, named Sam, was in Africa doing some contract work for a diamond company. There were a variety of other reasons, some legit, others bullshit—financial concerns, family problems, work, etc. I understood the hesitation. Coming to Kurdistan was a dangerous mission, but I'm convinced that the greatest cause of angst and hesitation was not ISIS itself, but the fact that we would be operating outside the official sanction of the state. Putting your life on the line in battle is one thing, but doing so without the weight of your own government backing you up is something entirely different.

Soldiers are like everyone else in the sense that we want to know we are doing the right thing. This affirmation comes from our own sense of justice, but also the knowledge that our government and people back home support whatever mission we are on. There's a comfort that comes with this, but in its absence, a soldier's only guide is his own conviction. That's what scares people the most. However, I knew I was in the right and that my mission was just. Perhaps my strident libertarianism was what allowed me to operate with a conviction that my mission was justifiable, even without some government official publicly patting me on the back. The lack of additional Western volunteers was a disappointment, but in hindsight, it should not have been a surprise.

There was an exception, though. From the very beginning of my correspondence with the members of Kerry Dragon's group, one man stood out from the rest for his keenness to join the fight against ISIS. Ethan is a Texan and a former American marine who had served a tour of duty in Iraq in 2006. During the previous months and weeks I had built up a pretty good rapport with Ethan and knew that he wasn't bullshitting when he said he was coming. While at the Sulaymaniyah Peshmerga base, I got a message that he had bought his ticket and a life insurance policy and was on his way. Of course the first American to be on the ground with the Peshmerga would be a Texan.

LIEUTENANT ALI AND I LEFT THE PESHMERGA BASE AND HEADED for Sulaymaniyah International Airport to pick up Ethan. We were both excited by the prospect of another Westerner—a marine, no less—joining our fledgling unit of foreign volunteers. The first of the passengers began filing through the automatic doors—mostly

Kurds, with the odd white face among them. Then we saw Ethan. He looked like I probably did when I arrived at the same airport the previous month: switched on and alert.

Fortunately for Ethan, his arrival was a smoother transition than mine. For starters, Lieutenant Ali and I were actually there to pick him up—unlike my arrival, where I was greeted by a stranger. Secondly, Ali had made the appropriate phone calls ahead of time to clear up any potential headaches and as a result, Ethan sailed through customs without even getting his bags scanned, which was good because he came to Kurdistan kitted out better than I was. The three of us drove back to base and got Ethan set up in our room.

When I first arrived on base a few weeks prior, I was a novelty and random Peshmerga soldiers would come over to see me and say hello. It was the same thing when Ethan arrived. He had a Velcro flag of Texas on his vest—every single Kurd recognized it. "Ah, Texas," they would say excitedly. "George Bush! Yes!" Seriously, virtually every Kurd knew the Texas state flag and could make the connection with former president George W. Bush. I'm also being serious when I say that I never met a Kurd who could identify the red-and-white Velcro maple leaf patch that I wore on my TAC vest. When pressed to make an educated guess about where Canada was on a map, the most common response was somewhere in Europe.

It's funny that as Canadians, we pride ourselves on being loved around the world, but truthfully, the world couldn't care less about Canada. I hope one day that we can all drop our sense of self-righteousness about how universally loved our country is. It isn't. If you go beyond the Western world, Canada doesn't exist.

‡‡‡

THERE WAS FIGHTING TAKING PLACE TO THE SOUTH IN JALULA, close to Baghdad, at this time. ISIS had been beaten, but there was still a mopping-up operation taking place and Ali had to rejoin his unit there. Ethan and I wanted to go, but Ali wanted Ethan to get acclimatized to his new surroundings and insisted we stay on base and wait for his return. That meant hanging around Sulaymaniyah for an indeterminate amount of time, though Ali promised we would go back to the front upon his return. There was nothing else to do except wait it out. I dicked around on my computer and Ethan worked out. He had even brought resistance cables and we built a dip bar to stay fit. I had left Canada in great shape, but already the diet of beans and rice was beginning to take its toll, and I could tell by brief looks in the mirror that I was losing muscle mass quickly.

The other officers kept up the tradition of taking us out for dinner at the local markets and visiting hookah bars, and though they didn't drink alcohol, they would gladly take us to beer stores and Ethan and I would crush a couple of cans before getting back to base. Sometimes we would go into Sulaymaniyah by ourselves, see the city and inevitably end up in a bar. It's funny to think of beer stores and bars in Iraq, but they do exist. In fact, Kurdish bars are on the whole better than what you would expect to find in Canada. There was one dive, but the rest were upscale, modern and classy, places where Western aid workers, teachers and rich, attractive Kurds could drink wine, spirits and European import beers like Tuborg and Heineken. It's civilized and the way things should be.

One night we got a little out of control and stumbled back to base. When we got to our quarters, there was a captain sharing Lieutenant Ali's room and he was offended that we stank like beer. The captain didn't say anything to us, but he ratted on Lieutenant

Ali to the Peshmerga chain of command. If his goal was to limit the number of people he had to share this spacious room with, his mission backfired. When Ali returned from Jalula, he freaked out at the captain and kicked him out of the room. The dressing-down of a senior officer was bewildering to me and Ethan, because quite frankly it would never have happened in the Canadian army or the marine corps. But this was Iraq and it's a strange war.

"How the hell do you get away with this?" I asked, and he said again that he creates and solves problems and people owed him favours.

As my mission in Kurdistan went on, I found that these words could just as easily be applied to me. It became more and more evident that my presence in Kurdistan was becoming a diplomatic and foreign-relations problem for the Kurds. A problem that was at least partially of Lieutenant Ali's own making.

The American and Canadian governments were putting increased pressure on the Kurdish government to punt Ethan and me from the front lines over fears that we might be captured or killed. In short, our own governments saw us as a liability. They didn't want screenshots of us in orange jumpsuits, from ISIS propaganda videos, ending up on the six o'clock news. This was a problem for the Kurds because they didn't want to ignore and potentially anger their powerful Western allies and backers. By keeping me more or less under his wing, Lieutenant Ali was fixing a problem for his chain of command.

It's a murky world that Ali operated in. I don't even know the half of it, but I'm sure glad he had our backs. I was also eager to hear what was happening in the various theatres of war, and Ali filled me in on what the situation was like in Jalula. In short, there had been a lot of heavy fighting with lots of casualties on both sides. However, they drove ISIS back and the city of about 100,000 had been liberated. It was the first major setback for ISIS, which made the victory all the more important. Yet it wasn't just the Kurds fighting ISIS. Iranian-backed Shia militias also played a significant role, and Lieutenant Ali recounted how, after the battle, the Shia fighters publicly beheaded a number of ISIS prisoners in a barbaric spectacle of bloodlust. You can say the jihadis deserved such a fate, and maybe they did, but I like to think we were better than that in the Peshmerga. ISIS prisoners were sometimes roughed up, but the Kurds never resorted to such barbarism. We treated our prisoners in this fashion and with a process of law, not because they deserved any form of mercy, but because it reminded us that we were better than the animals we fought against.

As far as I'm concerned, there is little difference in the moral ethos of either the Sunni-based ISIS or the Shia militias. ISIS may have the edge when it comes to committing heinous acts, but the Shia are not far behind. In this brutal region of Iraq, there is a harsh moral code that Westerners living in the comforts of North America will never understand, and believe me, you don't want to. This statement will offend a lot of readers, so all I can say is go over and see for yourself.

The Kurds understand this in a way that only an oppressed people can. For centuries they have been the targets of Arab aggression and ethnic cleansing, and in their minds ISIS is only the latest chapter in this existential struggle for survival. The liberation of Jalula posed a problem though for the Kurds, because the region is mixed demographically between Kurds and Arabs. The problem is that most of the Arabs were either tacitly complicit or outright supportive of ISIS, so what to do with them? The Kurdish answer was to impose restrictions on any Arab re-entering the captured territory if they could not prove that they had lived in the region before 1952. This essentially disqualified ninety per cent of the Arabs from returning. The remaining ten per cent had their homes bulldozed.

It sounds harsh, and it is. But compared to how ISIS operates in captured land, with rape, execution, torture, sex slaves and so on, the Kurdish policy seems progressive. The war against ISIS is an existential struggle for survival, and the stakes are too high to operate in any other way. If ISIS ever arrives back in the Jalula region, it will find that its once-fertile pool of recruits has dried up because the Arabs are gone.


SINCE MY ARRIVAL IN NOVEMBER, I HAD BEEN THE LONE WESTERN volunteer within the walls of the Sulaymaniyah Peshmerga base. Ethan's arrival had made it two Westerners. But now there were rumours of other American and Europeans who had shown up. Lieutenant Ali confirmed the rumour for us.

"Special forces?" I asked. The question drew a laugh from the lieutenant.

"No, no, just some clowns who got mixed up with the YPG in Syria. They aren't allowed on base, though," Ali explained.

It turns out that it's a small world for Western volunteers in the region, and before he had left stateside Ethan had been in contact with the same people Lieutenant Ali was speaking of. All we knew at the time was that these other Westerners had been in Syria, but apparently something had driven them to Iraq. We checked into it and Ethan made plans for a rendezvous with his countrymen.

Through the armed checkpoint on base, we drove into Sulaymaniyah and headed for a sports bar to meet up with the newly arrived gang of Westerners. I know what you are thinking: yes, there are sports bars in Kurdistan, but they play soccer and cricket on the screens rather than real sports like hockey. In fact, besides sports bars you can also find German- and Italian-themed restaurants in Kurdistan and even Irish pubs. The best part is that they all serve beer. I was curious to meet some fellow volunteers and knew we had reached the right place when I saw a couple of white guys and a Mexican sitting at a table. They gave us surprised looks when they saw us.

When you are a minority in a foreign land, you can always feel yourself sticking out like a sore thumb, and it doesn't matter how hospitable your hosts are. Even though it flies in the face of liberal and progressive attitudes, people find comfort in being around their own kind, especially when in a foreign land. It's just human nature. We introduced ourselves and I think we were all at least somewhat happy to know that we weren't the only Westerners in the city.

Sitting at a table off to one corner was James, ex–U.S. Army. Beside him was Juan, a Mexican-American and a former marine. The next man was named Hans, ex-Austrian army. They had three other companions somewhere in the city, but I got the vibe that they were reluctant to divulge too much information about themselves at the moment, though it turned out that they had quite the story to tell.

"Getting into Syria was easy. Leaving was the hard part." James spoke over a round of cold beer as the five of us sat around a table. Ethan and I had ditched our military attire and wore civvies, but we nonetheless received curious looks from the locals and expats in the establishment who could probably piece together what four white guys and a Mexican in their twenties and thirties

A platoon photo before we left Afghanistan,
around Remembrance Day 2014.

I was very angry at the time
this photo was taken, and I
thought to myself, *This is
not what I signed up for.*

The beautiful mountains above Sulaymaniyah,
where my adventures in Iraq would begin.

At the Peshmerga base in Sulaymaniyah shortly after my arrival. I sported my beret to show regimental pride in the PPCLI, although I was no longer an active member.

A makeshift forward operating base occupied by both the PKK and the Peshmerga, south of Kirkuk.

A crudely fashioned tank made from heavy machinery, which I nicknamed "the Kill-Dozer."

Driving to the staging area outside Kirkuk before the battle of Tal al-Ward, 26 November 2014. The gentleman sitting next to me is Brothahan. Hours later he was shot in the face during combat.

Arriving at the staging area across the bridge from Tal al-Ward. Katyusha rockets rained down on the ISIS positions.

A burning oil pipeline as seen from the newly captured ridge at Tal al-Ward.

Me (left) with two Peshmerga I had teamed up with during the fight at Tal al-Ward.

Pulling off the ridge at Tal al-Ward. I had lent
this fighter (far right) my British army desert smock.

Loading our gear into the bucket of a truck at Tal al-Ward.

Peshmerga mobile artillery at the Kirkuk train station.

Enjoying the sun at Rashad, northeast of Al-Fallujah, before the shooting started.

Taking a break at Rashad during a lull in the fighting.

Patrolling the front in the Daquq district in the back of a Toyota.

A Russian-made S-60, a 57-millimetre anti-aircraft gun, at a Daquq strongpoint. I loved seeing this weapons platform in action.

Ethan, General Araz and me on the Daquq front.

Manning the trenches of Arabcoy.

Keeping low to avoid ISIS snipers
on the Daquq front.

Drinking chai with the officers at a Daquq chai shop.

Ethan (right) and me with a Peshmerga fighter
on the night of a big battle in Daquq.

With Sheik Jaffer at his headquarters,
days prior to my departure.

Deep in thought after an artillery strike on the
Daquq front, shortly after 105-millimetre
shells had landed 50 metres away.

were doing in Kurdistan. Regardless, James spoke openly about their foray into Syria. The three of them had arrived in Kurdistan shortly after me and had made their way into Syria with another guy named Arman. Arman was a German national of Kurdish descent and also a member of the Median Empire, a European biker gang.

"Arman organized our rendezvous with the YPG, but things went to shit quickly," James continued. "Arman was under the impression that the four of us would be placed in a unit with other Westerners, but as soon as the YPG had us on their base, we were told that we would be split up for training purposes."

"We told them to fuck off," Hans piped up in his Austrian accent.

"Anyway, they kept us on base for one night, then dropped us off in the middle of nowhere and told us to hold the line. We were sitting ducks, though, because we had no support and no heavy weapons." So far, nothing James told me came as any surprise. The Peshmerga had told me often that the YPG were a bunch of amateurs, and James seemed to confirm this.

"Eventually, we left," said Hans. It wasn't the first time Hans had quit an army. He had deserted from the Austrian military and then tried to enlist in the French Foreign Legion; however, he was turned away because, contrary to popular belief, the Legion doesn't take just anybody and they certainly don't take deserters from foreign armies. Not that I could blame these guys for quitting their post. The situation as described by James seemed absurd. A handful of Westerners with no support and alone on the front was a recipe for disaster. I wasn't surprised, though, because as messed up as things could be in Iraq, it didn't compare to Syria. The Kurdish YPG in Syria is an offshoot of the Iraq-based PKK (they are essentially the same organization) and I knew full well what it was like being attached to them.

James and the guys hiked to a nearby town and then bought a ride to what used to be the Iraq–Syria border. Once they crossed over into Kurdistan, they were taken into custody at a Peshmerga checkpoint.

"To give Arman credit, he did get us out of that mess, but we've been held at arm's length from the Peshmerga since then," James said.

"Yeah, we heard you guys weren't allowed to enter the base."

"It's true. But Arman says he can get things sorted out with the Pesh. Might just take some time."

From what I gathered, this Arman guy figured that because he was Kurdish, he could basically do whatever he wanted, which included recruiting Westerners into his own unaffiliated gang. But instead of the red-carpet treatment, the Peshmerga were keeping a close eye on him and everyone else associated with him.

I GOT A CALL FROM HANS A FEW DAYS LATER. OVER BEER IN Sulaymaniyah, I had told the guys about my stint with the PKK, and now the Austrian was on my case, wanting to know how he could join their ranks. Hans is a switched-on soldier. The way he tells it, he left the Austrian army because he knew there was no chance in hell of ever being used in combat. Trying to enlist in the French Foreign Legion was a logical choice for someone wanting to fight, but since that didn't work out as planned, he went to the Ukraine and fought alongside pro-Kiev forces against Russian soldiers. I got the impression that Hans sees himself as a European patriot, but if there is one thing more worthwhile than fighting the Russians, it's fighting the jihadist hordes of the Islamic Caliphate. When ISIS burst onto the scene, Hans packed his bags and said his goodbyes to his Ukrainian friends and then jumped on a plane to Kurdistan.

The abortive Syrian foray had left a bad taste in his mouth and he wanted out of Arman's group and away from Sulaymaniyah.

"Can you hook me up with the PKK?"

"Yeah, but the YPG and the PKK are the same. If you didn't like the YPG in Syria, you probably won't like PKK," I cautioned him. I listed off a whole host of reasons why it was a bad idea to link up with the PKK: they kill civilians, they are undisciplined, they are communist. "You can't just walk away from the PKK. The first thing they will do is take your phone away and you'll be stranded." I was starting to sound like my older brother when he tried to convince me not to come to Iraq. The Austrian was unmoved. He was like me—he had come to Kurdistan to fight ISIS, and for better or worse, the PKK was his best bet. I gave him the contact information for PKK Ali.

"You are going to regret this," I warned him, but his mind was made up, and the next day he left Sulaymaniyah.

I heard from Hans about a month later. He said, "You were right." Everything I had warned him about the PKK had proven true. They confiscated his phone and electronic devices, as I said they would, but things got even worse. Somehow the PKK had found out that Hans had deserted from the YPG in Syria, and because the two groups are so closely intertwined, they weren't happy about it. Hans was kept under lockdown, with no weapon and no way to call for help. Whereas I was a guest who couldn't leave the PKK, Hans was a flat-out prisoner. Thankfully, I had Lieutenant Ali to bail me out of my predicament, but the Austrian was on his own. It got to a point where he thought his life was in real danger, but like I said before, Hans is a switched-on mother. And resourceful. In the dark of night, he jumped out of a two-storey window and struck out on his own cross-country. He left all of his gear behind and travelled light, and the next day he came upon a town and a Peshmerga checkpoint, which was his salvation. Soon afterwards, Hans was back fighting in the Ukraine.

### 14 DECEMBER 2014

"LET'S GO." ALI WAS HAPPY AND ENTHUSIASTIC, BUT IT WAS nothing compared to how Ethan and I felt at the news we were shipping out to Kirkuk and the front. I didn't know how long I would be gone, so I packed everything except my civilian clothes and loaded my bags into the white Toyota. The highway leading west from Sulaymaniyah was by now familiar to me and we drove past small towns and villages that were nestled into the Kurdish mountains. These peaks weren't as dramatic as the Canadian Rockies, but they were partially covered in snow and reminded me of the drive from Calgary to the ski resorts at Banff and Lake Louise.

The highway turned and we started heading south through the arid flatlands towards the front. I was stoked to be getting back into the action and I gave Ethan a rundown on what it was like and the things he would see. He had heard it all before, but it is more real to talk about these things when you are travelling at 180 kilometres an hour towards enemy lines, rather than hanging out in garrison.

We drove through Kirkuk without stopping and then took Highway 3 to an abandoned train station about thirty kilometres south of the city. The tracks were still there, but their disuse was apparent. The station itself was dilapidated, but it served as the Peshmerga headquarters for the sector we were in. There were about two hundred Peshmerga soldiers here and an unusual amount of heavy weaponry, including mobile artillery and enormous heavy trucks with 57-millimetre anti-aircraft cannons mounted on the back. Like the Germans in the Second World War, the Kurds have modified these guns to shoot at ground forces, instead of at targets in the air. Once again, it's necessity that drives this destructive creativity, because when an ISIS tanker truck full of oil and explosives is barrelling towards your position, there's no point having cannons pointing in the air.

Lieutenant Ali introduced Ethan and me to the ranking general at the FOB. He spoke English, as many of the senior ranks do, and showered us with praise for helping his people fight ISIS. More important, he agreed that Ethan and I could go to the front. The districts south of Kirkuk were alive with offensives and counterattacks, and the general promised us we would see action. We said goodbye to Ali as he left to rejoin his unit and then spent the night in the station. We woke early the next morning to eggs and bread, filled our canteens with warm water and then headed for the front.

# 13.

# RASHAD

15 DECEMBER 2014

ETHAN AND I WERE DEPLOYED TO RASHAD, A SMALL VILLAGE IN the barren wastelands between Kurdistan and Iraq. Beyond a small cluster of decrepit homes made of bullet-torn concrete blocks, there is nothing there except war. It's simply a place name on a map along Highway 24, forty kilometres south of Kirkuk. If you were to keep travelling south, you would eventually come to the city of Tikrit, hometown of former Iraqi dictator Saddam Hussein. But it's impossible to make that drive under current circumstances because ISIS is in the way and the black flags of the Caliphate fly menacingly over the abandoned hovels that line the road. The trenches on the front lines of the war cut across the edge of Rashad.

I had a sense of déjà vu on arriving at Rashad—the similarities with Tal al-Ward were uncanny. The size of the two villages was similar (Rashad was a little smaller), and even the river running slowly along its border was the same. A man could take a piss in the river at Tal al-Ward and it would slowly flow downstream in the stagnant water to Rashad. Defensive berms lined both sides of the river, and of course there was only one way to cross: a bridge fifteen metres long that separated the combatants.

"This is just like Tal al-Ward," I said to Ethan, and he nodded his head, familiar with the stories I had told of my first battle.

The bridge was a post-apocalyptic sight and we stared at the craters, mines and barbed wire that covered the structure. At the far end, bunkers and sandbag redoubts tipped with black flags marked the jihadi strongpoints that guarded the one entrance into Rashad. Both sides had their machine guns trained along the length of the bridge, and neither ISIS nor the Peshmerga had any intention of forcing a crossing over its beams. The Kurds were content to simply hold their side of the bridge, and apparently the jihadis felt the same way.

We disembarked from the truck and moved into the labyrinth of trenches, bunkers and sandbag walls of the Kurdish lines. There were around 150 Peshmerga embedded in the fortifications, but they were keeping their heads down, smoking and taking only occasional glances through the gaps in the sandbag walls that allowed us to spy on the enemy. The tension that comes from war hung in the air, but by and large it was a laid-back atmosphere.

Yet not all was quiet along the front. It was Iraq, after all, and the shit is never too far away in this land of perpetual war. A major battle was brewing about five kilometres north of our location. Ethan and I sat in our designated bunker, listening to rocket and artillery detonations in the distance, accompanied by the rattle of small-arms fire. Our blood was already up from being just a stone's throw away from the enemy, and the sound of battle only heightened our wish that the fighting would shift to our sector. Another massive thud sounded in the distance, followed by two more in quick succession. It was enough to make the Kurds sharing our bunker pause for a brief moment before casually resuming their cigarettes and conversation.

We took turns peering out from an observation hole left open in the sandbag wall and checking out the enemy positions. They were formidable. As deadly as the bridge at Tal al-Ward had been, it paled in comparison to this. Attempting a crossing over this bridge into Rashad would be nearly suicidal, but still, Ethan and I were hopeful we would have a go at it. But the Kurds dismissed the idea of launching an attack out of hand. "No, no, no," one of them said. It was probably the only word of English that he knew, yet he said it quite emphatically.

We kept scanning the enemy works, but the jihadis were being smart and did not offer any targets. To the enemy's credit, their defences were properly constructed, and so the only glimpses of ISIS that Ethan and I could see were enemy trucks coming to and from the village. Yet they were beyond the effective distance of our rifles.

"God, I hope this battle comes our way," I said aloud at the sound of another explosion.

"Damn right," Ethan answered. At that moment, another Kurdish soldier entered the bunker. He was about my age, small and wiry, with a switched-on look in his eyes. The markings on his uniform showed that he was an officer, and the Peshmerga soldiers raised their gaze to him, waiting for an order that did not come. That's because he had come to see the two Westerners who had arrived.

"Hello. I'm Lieutenant Dan," he said in a Kurdish (with a hint of British) accent.

Ethan and I looked at each other with puzzled faces.

"*Who* are you?" Ethan asked.

"Lieutenant Dan." The man spoke even more deliberately than before, in near-perfect English. I looked at Ethan again and there was a grin on his face. We both suppressed the involuntary chuckle that comes from meeting a Kurdish soldier named Lieutenant Dan in the middle of Iraq. Lieutenant Dan, just like the character from *Forrest Gump*. I doubted this wiry soldier had ever seen the film. He shook our hands and, as was so often the case with the Peshmerga, expressed his thanks that we had flown halfway across the world to fight ISIS. "Please come with me," he said, and we picked up our rifles and followed him out of the bunker and into the trench system.

We stopped at an observation point and he let us use a scope that he pulled from a pocket. "Look over the bridge. You see the two concrete bunkers? ISIS is in there with machine guns. Now look just past the village where the road dips down. They have a mortar there." Lieutenant Dan pointed out some more of the many challenges facing the Peshmerga across the river and I handed the scope to Ethan, who took it all in with a soldier's watchful eye. "Fucking terrorists," Dan said as he pointed out another enemy bunker. "This is a shitty little village, but if we don't hold them here, the jihadis will spread to the next shitty little village, and the next and the next, and soon they will be at Kirkuk's doorstep. We almost lost the city a few months ago."

"That's why we came," I said.

Dan broke out in a smile. "I'm glad you did. I heard about you at Tal al-Ward," he said while leading us towards the de facto command post. "You were in *Rudaw News* and people talk. Hopefully, there will be more of you coming." By this point I doubted many more Westerners with military experience would come, but I didn't say anything.

The command post had a few chairs, a sofa, a table, a TV, maps and, most important, cold water and soda. Dan showed us a map of the area and pointed with his index finger to the spot where the loud artillery thuds were coming from. I forget the name of the place, but it was a small outpost of habitation like Rashad. "Daesh attacked and now we are counterattacking. That's what you are hearing," he said while tapping at the location on the map.

"Are we going to attack?" I asked while trying to subdue the hopefulness in my voice. I desperately wanted to fire my rifle at the enemy again and was getting impatient. Ethan felt the same way, perhaps more so given that his visa would expire before mine. "No, my friend. Not today. But I wish we could."

"Let's fucking do it, then." In hindsight, it's funny that we could talk military strategy with Kurdish officers, but we did so frequently because they held Western soldiers in such high regard. Lieutenant Dan was no exception, and he projected an atmosphere of mutual trust and respect from the moment we met him.

"You want to be the first man across the bridge?" he asked. "We'll lose half our men if we try." He was probably right. "But still, I would love to get into Rashad like my cock wants to get into a pussy." The expression was funny—funnier still when said in a Kurdish accent—and the three of us laughed together and smoked while looking at the map. "If we can break ISIS here," said Dan as he pointed to the location of the current battle, "then we can outflank Rashad and not need to cross the bridge." The battle north of us made a lot more sense now. Prying ISIS out of Rashad via a flanking movement would undoubtedly cost fewer lives than storming the bridge.

Still, Ethan and I pressed our case. "The enemy is distracted now. It's the perfect time to attack when their forces are busy fighting north."

Dan grunted. "Maybe so," he said. "I'm not in charge, anyway. The general would have to order an attack."

"Would you order the attack if you could?" Ethan asked.

"Of course." If asked a few hours before, I doubt Lieutenant Dan would have responded the same way, but he was feeding off of our enthusiasm. "But the generals won't go for it."

"Maybe we can find another way to get at them," I suggested.

"There's just one bridge—"

"We don't need the bridge," interrupted Ethan. "We could wait until night and then cross the river. How deep is it?"

"Up to your chest," Dan answered. "We could get across without getting our guns wet." He was becoming animated now. "But we'll bring knives too and use those to take out their sentries first. Nice and quiet." Dan revealed an impressive steel blade. I carried a combat knife, too. If you ever have to kill with a knife, it probably means that your mission is completely messed up, but they are good to have just in case. "Once we clear their bunkers, we'll give a call sign and the rest of our forces can attack across the bridge." Dan concluded the sketch of his wild plan.

"Let's get cammed up." I didn't have any face paint but maybe someone else did. Ethan didn't, neither did Dan, and I would bet a hundred bucks that nobody in the entire command had any. Dan would be fine with his brown skin, but Ethan and I could just use the stinking mud from the riverbank to cover our pale faces. That would do just as well. The only problem was that, just like in the movie *Forrest Gump*, the Kurdish Lieutenant Dan was a little crazy. I say that in a good way—you need to be a little crazy to be a good soldier—but when he started talking about making a ghillie suit and carrying that across the river too, it became apparent that the entire conversation was simply a flight of fancy. There would be no commando-style raid on the enemy with cold steel, though Ethan and I would have gone if there were a serious plan in place. Instead, we chilled with Dan for a while longer and then the three of us resumed our post in the trenches.

It was a classic stalemate scenario in the trenches. The detonations marking the battle north were still audible, but Rashad was quiet. No movement, no shots fired, no nothing. I scoped the enemy works with my rifle, but there were simply no targets to fire at. It's a common misconception that opposing armies will automatically fire on each other if in range. But it's not the reality. Unless there is an offensive, there is little shooting, save for the occasional sniping. Constantly engaging the enemy would be a colossal waste of resources. The Arabs often fire their weapons into the air in a laughable expression of bravado, but ammunition is expensive and constantly in short supply. As in the Canadian army, the Kurds don't waste their ammunition. They have something that is rare in this part of the world: discipline.

I imagined the stalemate at Rashad was much the same as life in the trenches during the First World War, with soldiers content to keep their heads down and their rifles idle. My great-grandfather was an officer with the Canadian army in that war and was shot through the hand, which for the rest of his life remained clenched in a fist due to the nerve damage. The incapacitating wound took him from the front and probably saved his life.

But the quiet was not to last. It was Iraq and the shit was never too far away. Actually, it was just around the corner in the form of a pickup truck and a few PKK fighters intent on stirring things up at the front.

## 15 DECEMBER 2014
## 1600 HRS

THE TRUCK ROLLED UP CLOSE TO OUR POSITION AND FOUR Kurds disembarked. They had the usual small arms—Kalashnikovs— but one of them carried a homemade .50-calibre sniper rifle. We watched from the trenches as they set up the long-distance killer and trained it on the enemy lines. The Peshmerga and PKK will come together and coordinate their activities on occasion, but not all the time. This was one of the times when the Peshmerga had no idea what their Marxist cousins in the PKK were up to, and Lieutenant Dan only shrugged his shoulders when I asked what was going on.

*Bang!* The .50-calibre rifle fired and the first round struck one of the ISIS concrete bunkers on the far side of the bridge. A puff of white dust marked where the bullet had penetrated. *Bang!* Again, fresh dust exploded from the concrete. The bunker was an easy target and the PKK could have easily peppered the enemy strongpoint with their Kalashnikovs, but it would have done no good. Instead, they deployed the sniper rifle—not because they needed precision, but because the .50-calibre round was beastly enough to smash through the thick bunker's walls. *Bang!* The third round bored another hole through the enemy position.

*Zip. Zip. Zip.* The PKK had disturbed the hornet's nest and the enemy wasted little time in firing back at our trenches. We were protected within our sandbag walls but instinctively ducked lower while listening to the jihadi bullets that buzzed over our heads like a swarm of angry hornets. "Fuckers!" Lieutenant Dan cursed in English for our benefit, but he wasn't referring to ISIS, who were trying to kill us. His anger, like the rest of the Peshmerga, was directed at the PKK who had started an unwanted fight with the jihadis.

*Bang!* The next .50-calibre round smacked into the concrete bunker and now the swooshing and zipping noises of the enemy bullets filled the air thicker than before. The Kurds manned their battle stations, poking rifle barrels through the gaps and slits in the sandbag fortifications. Some of the Peshmerga began firing back across the river, but they were quickly called off by their officers and sergeants. ISIS wasn't presenting any targets, so firing rounds at this point was simply a waste of ammunition. Judging by the incoming fire, ISIS seemed to have an unlimited supply of ammo. Mortars too.

The first of the enemy projectiles began plunging from the sky and rocked our position. It was death from above and we hurried into areas that were less exposed to the jihadi mortar fire. There was a loud explosion close by, followed by the screaming of an unlucky man who had taken a lump of shrapnel to his hand. The hand was still attached to the arm, but it was badly mangled and there wasn't enough left to make a proper fist with. No doubt the war would be over for him, just like it was for my great-grandfather a hundred years ago.

Taking a wound like that from a mortar doesn't make you a bad soldier; it's simply a case of being in the wrong place at the wrong time. It's fate and luck, rather than a reflection on individual soldiering skills. This man was simply unlucky.

*Bang!* The sniper rifle was still in action as mortar rounds kept falling. I looked out across the river to Rashad and could see the area where the mortar fire was coming from. They were close and had set up in a depression in the terrain, which kept them from our view. In the military we call this "dead ground," or an area of the battlefield that you can't see due to the contours of the land. ISIS was taking advantage of this concept and was protected from our rifle fire. However, they were a little too close for their own good.

It seems counterintuitive, but to fire a mortar accurately, it's better to be farther away from your target than closer. Thankfully, the proximity of the jihadis to our own lines was a detriment to their weapons' effectiveness and they couldn't get a solid trajectory on us. Nevertheless, the danger was still real and the only way we could hit back was with Katyusha rockets and artillery.

*Bang!* The PKK had essentially destroyed the enemy bunker and they began packing up their gear, including the improvised sniper rifle, and then loaded back into the truck. They peeled off from the front in a cloud of dust and left us to deal with the fallout of their raid. Kurdish rockets and artillery started screaming overhead and landed among the enemy works and rear staging areas. The sounds of war are exhilarating once you get over the initial shock, and I watched as smoke billowed up from across the river where our ordnance had made impact. ISIS small-arms fire slackened in response and the skirmish at Rashad transitioned into a long-range duel between Kurdish rockets and ISIS mortars that drowned out the larger battle still raging eight kilometres farther north.

There was a section of the line that had received a few direct hits, and Lieutenant Dan wanted to check out the damage. The three of us waited for a break in the incoming and then left the bunker that we were holed up in. The trenches were a labyrinth of zigzagging sandbag walls, and so we decided to break from the fortifications and move straight along the protected side of the berm to save time. In so doing, we let our guard down for the foolish reason of saving a few minutes on a nonessential recce.

An enemy mortar landed on our side of the berm and exploded about thirty metres from where we stood. The shock wave shook me up. I could feel the explosive energy passing through my body and it took my breath away. Dan and Ethan dove for the ground, as was the smart thing to do to avoid the shrapnel, but I stood still, reactionless and in awe of what I had just seen. I was like a stunned idiot. *Oh shit, my reflexes are bad*, I thought to myself when the dust settled. Ethan and Dan rose from the ground and we quickly checked ourselves for wounds. At thirty metres a mortar could kill you, but it's unlikely, and thankfully we were fine, if a little shaken.

Throughout the rest of the day and into the early evening the rounds from both sides continued shrieking overhead. We fired our rifles a few times, purely out of boredom, frustration and the joy that comes from losing rounds on the enemy, even though we knew that we wouldn't hit anyone. After a while I put my rifle aside and just watched the front, specifically the area that we knew the mortars were coming from. It was the right moment to look, and I saw an amazing thing happen. I'm not sure if it was a rocket or artillery, but something detonated directly in the dead ground where we figured the mortar team was concealed. The earth exploded, smoke rose, and for the first time in hours, the enemy mortars went silent.


WE STAYED THE NIGHT IN THE LINES LOOKING OUT OVER RASHAD, but the front had returned to its normal state of quiet readiness and alert. The guns and weaponry had fallen silent. Even the sounds of battle to the north had ended. I have no idea who won that fight, but no doubt there were casualties. If the Kurds lost one man, then ISIS likely lost two or three, and that doesn't even include the jihadis taken out by coalition air strikes. It's not unusual for ISIS fighters to go into combat hopped up on all kinds of drugs. It makes them fearless, but also stupid, and the Kurds make them pay for their artificial courage with a favourable body count ratio. The only problem is that ISIS often outnumbers the Kurds and can afford to be reckless with the lives of its fighters. It's easy to do when you believe the dead go directly to heaven, where seventy-two virgins are waiting. The Kurds don't share this belief, and the need to conserve manpower as well as their own moral code prevents a casual waste of lives.

"This is what we'll do tomorrow." Night had fallen and Ethan and I were back at the command post with Lieutenant Dan, who had come up with another plan. But he was being serious this time and more realistic than going on a knife-wielding raid across the river at night. There were a few buildings on our side of the river and Dan suggested that we go up on the roofs to snipe at the enemy. I liked the plan and discussed it further with Ethan as we went to our quarters for the night. We were lucky; we got to sleep in a centralized housing unit, which is a fancy way of saying that we slept in a shipping container that had been brought to the front for such purposes. Sea Cans are a cheap and easy way to house soldiers, and they are a common sight just behind the trenches. In more elaborate cases, multiple Sea Cans are joined together, sometimes stacked one on top of the other. Then you have a Sea Can house.

‡‡‡

I WAS HAVING A BREAKFAST OF BEANS, RICE AND BREAD WITH
Ethan and a few Peshmerga when Lieutenant Dan's phone rang. It
was Lieutenant Ali. Dan looked at me with the phone held to his
ear and I could see disappointment on his face. Ethan and I had
to leave. Yesterday's fighting had spooked the general in charge
of the Rashad sector. "He doesn't want you killed on his watch,"
Dan said. I wasn't surprised. If Ethan or I had been captured or
killed, it would be a political embarrassment and a black eye for
the Kurdish government. All I wanted to do was continue the fight
against ISIS, but the political risks posed by my presence were
becoming more apparent. The Canadian government was leaning heavily on the Kurdistan Regional Government to release me
from service, and if the worst happened, the general responsible
would be hung out to dry. Nevertheless, there was another general
who was willing to take us on.

Lieutenant Ali drove from Kirkuk and picked us up. I didn't
try to hide my disappointment and frustration at being pulled
from the front, because it was bullshit. I didn't come here to play
soldier behind the lines.

"I know, I know." Ali didn't like the situation either. "Things
will work out. General Araz is hardcore and doesn't give a fuck
about the politics," he answered.

In the Peshmerga, each general has a lot of autonomy, much
more so than a general in the Canadian army. They choose who is
in their units and who is out.

"General Araz is hardcore. He leads from the front and he
wants you guys with him." Ali told us more about Araz as he drove
towards the commander's headquarters at the town of Daquq,
about forty kilometres south of Kirkuk on Highway 3. Araz had
been a general in the reconstituted Iraqi national army after the

toppling of Saddam Hussein. Yet when the Iraqis fled Mosul and left Kirkuk wide open to ISIS, Araz joined the only force on the ground that could stand up to the jihadis. That's why he commanded a brigade of Peshmerga in the Daquq district.

We found Araz in an abandoned school that had been turned into a brigade headquarters. It was a grand setup, at least for this part of the world. There were tiled floors, nice, comfortable chairs and a corporal who acted as a butler. The room was filled with smoke and every time one of the generals stubbed out a cigarette, the corporal would dutifully empty the ashtray, clean it and then return it to whatever side table it had been taken from. Ali, Ethan and I sat down and were immediately offered cold water and soda by the corporal.

We drank our drinks and waited as Araz and the half dozen other generals and officers in the room discussed something in their own language. Araz could speak broken English and even some Swedish. His wife was a Swede and his children were schooled in that Nordic country. After an hour, Ethan and I were brought into the conversation. Araz seemed like a good guy, and he asked us questions about our past military experience and why we had come to his country.

"To kill ISIS," we said, and they seemed to like that.

"You can come with us," General Araz said, meaning that we could join his unit. "But I need two days to get things sorted out. In the meantime, my driver will take you to Sulaymaniyah. I'll call you when we are ready to pick you up."

I left Daquq with a happy heart, confident that I would be back with a unit that was ready to fight and a commander who wanted my services. I would enjoy my two days in Sulaymaniyah and then be back in action.

# 14.

# WAITING FOR WAR

17 DECEMBER 2014
SULAYMANIYAH, KURDISTAN
WHILE GENERAL ARAZ GOT THINGS SORTED OUT, WHATEVER that meant, Ethan and I waited for his call in a Sulaymaniyah hotel. With a million and a half inhabitants, Sulaymaniyah is paired with Erbil as the two biggest cities in Kurdistan. In many ways Sulaymaniyah is a modern city—not quite what you would find in Canada, but at the same time more than you would expect to see in Iraq. There are large buildings, lush parks, multilane highways, fancy restaurants and even a five-star hotel that was well beyond our financial reach. We had both paid our own way to Kurdistan and the cost had been heavy for both of us. With limited funds, necessity demanded that we settle into a really crappy hotel room. The heater didn't work and, contrary to popular belief, there are parts of Iraq that get cold in winter. The showers barely worked, and of course there were no towels. The entire hotel had a dim, dingy and dirty feel. I wish I could remember the name of the

place so as to give warning to other Westerners not to go there. But I didn't really have a choice. It was the only place Ethan and I could afford. And we had both slept in far worse conditions.

We knew we had two days, so we planned to make the most of our time there. And by that, I mean drinking, picking up women and enjoying life in a strange land. On our first night we decided to get out of our shitty hotel room and visit the Grand Millennium Hotel.

The Grand Millennium is the tallest structure in Kurdistan and an iconic fixture of the Sulaymaniyah skyline. At night, the hotel is flooded in blue lights, which reflect off the countless glass windows that cover its sides. It's the first thing I noticed flying into the city and you simply can't miss it. The hotel is modern, cosmopolitan, clean and a magnet for rich Kurds and Westerners alike. We ate at a nice Italian restaurant and then headed to the lounge, which seemed to have attracted all the white women in the country. But we were getting shot down left, right and centre.

It was a bit of a shock to us, because up to this point we had been treated like kings everywhere we went. You would assume that two robust white guys would clean up in a place like Kurdistan. Hell, I had half-expected to be invited into homes to marry daughters. But I couldn't have been more wrong. The Western women were an assortment of self-righteous liberal humanitarian workers who wanted nothing to do with Ethan and me. We were beneath them and only slightly better than the jihadis we were fighting against. The men in the bar treated us with the same indifference. These were the wealthy elite of Kurdish society and they were content to sip cocktails and drinks while the Peshmerga held ISIS at the gates. The Peshmerga soldiers often go months without getting paid, and yet, whenever I needed something, they would pay out of pocket without hesitation and force me to put my wallet away. They genuinely appreciated my presence because they knew the sacrifices I had made to fight alongside them. The pricks at the Grand Millennium served as the perfect contrast to the selflessness of the average Peshmerga soldier, who was fighting to protect his country and family from the Caliphate's brutality. So long as someone else was doing the fighting, the patrons of the hotel would be fine and wouldn't have to lift a finger for their own country's defence.

The local women were a little more receptive. Ethan and I chatted up a pair of good-looking girls and I got a number. Things were looking good. Unfortunately, Ethan was not having any luck with the woman he was interested in. He couldn't get her number.

"Dillon, give me your girl's number so that I can contact her and get her friend's number later."

"No way, man," I said. "These are Kurdish girls, not Texas broads. She'll be pissed if I give you her number."

"Come on, son."

I knew she would be pissed, but I sent him her number anyway, if for no other reason than to stop the bitching. I was right, though: she was *pissed* when she found out.

"Never give out my number," she said acidly and then turned her back on me. I played that one wrong. No matter; there were more women at the bar and we both ended up staying the night in the Grand Millennium. It was a pretentious, stuck-up place, but we had our fun and were able to tick off the items on our list.

*Good food. Check.*
*Drinks. Check.*
*Women. Check.*

Odd coincidences sometimes come up in life, but when they occur in a strange land like Iraq they are more profound. Ethan and I crawled back to our less-than-five-star hotel the next morning. We were hurting pretty bad from the self-inflicted wounds of having too much alcohol, but we still had one more night of freedom. I had earlier received a Facebook message from a girl named Heather, who was in Erbil. Not only was she Canadian, but she was from the same small town I grew up in. Carleton Place is about forty minutes from Ottawa, with a population of about ten thousand. The odds that someone else from Carleton Place was in Kurdistan took me by surprise. Heather is a few years younger than I am. I had never met her before, but a quick look at her Facebook profile showed that we had some mutual connections. She was also very attractive and wanted to meet up. I couldn't say no. Heather was in Erbil and we were in Suli, but that was a minor detail. I dragged Ethan with me and we hopped into a Corolla that had been converted into a cab. Two hours and fifty dollars later, we were in Erbil, the capital of the Kurdistan Region.

We arrived later in the day and checked into a nice hotel, the kind you might expect to find in Canada. It was in the Christian district of Erbil, which is where you want to be. It's a common misconception that there are no Christians in the Middle East, yet Christianity has been present in this part of the world longer than Islam. Most major cities have a Christian quarter or district, and there are entire regions and towns that have Christian majorities. That's not to say that Christianity is by any means a dominant religious force in the region. In fact, the religion is becoming weaker with every passing year. It's ironic that Christians enjoyed more protection under Saddam Hussein than under current circumstances. Saddam was a brutal tyrant, but he was largely secular, and so Christians as a group were not persecuted any more than other sects. ISIS, and to a lesser extent the Shia-led government in Baghdad, has driven many of the region's Christians into the only safe space left to them: Kurdistan.

One of the great things about the Christian quarter of Erbil is that it has numerous bars and restaurants where you can enjoy a leisurely beer. There's even a German-style restaurant in the area. We went out for a few beers (okay, maybe it was a little more than a few), and in typical Texas fashion Ethan got loaded. I joked with him that he could handle only the watery piss that Americans are used to. I'm going to spare Ethan the embarrassment by not getting into the details of the night, but it was a fun time.

The next day, I met up with Heather. She came to our hotel room and the two of us went to a nearby hookah bar. It was a classy, well-lit establishment and we smoked some lemon shisha together. I admit that it was great being with a girl from back home and we hit it off, despite her being a left-wing idealist. We had some good laughs and I told her about the cold shoulder Ethan and I had gotten from other Western girls in country.

"It's because they are self-righteous and your presence makes them confront their own hypocrisy." I let her continue because I didn't understand what she was getting at.

"Listen," she said, "these girls come over here for a few months to teach or do some other volunteer work and everyone from back home tells them what a great humanitarian job they are doing. I know, because I'm one of them. But they aren't really doing anything, especially compared to what you came here for. You are making an actual difference and they resent it."

Heather had some great stories about being in the Pakistani tribal areas and was well travelled. Unfortunately, I never saw her again, but I hope she is doing well. I especially appreciated Heather's insight into the psychology of Western aid workers in country. I'm not sure if it was true for everyone, but it was definitely accurate at least to some degree, which was apparent with the next group of Westerners we met.

A driver from the hotel in Erbil took us back to Suli. Like most Peshmerga, he did two-week stints at the front in uniform and then had two weeks off, during which he resumed his civilian job as a driver. Like Lieutenant Ali, our driver was in the intelligence branch of the Peshmerga, and he drove like an absolute maniac. Speed was of no concern to him and whenever we approached a checkpoint he simply flashed his military ID and then sped onward. At one stop, there was a long line of Arabs waiting in their cars and our driver simply drove over the median and onto the opposing lane to skip the queue. He cursed at the Arabs who had slowed us down for a fraction of a second and then sped onward. He had us back to Sulaymaniyah in record time. Unfortunately, we arrived to depressing news. We were expecting to rejoin General Araz at the front, but he called me that day to say that he was no longer sure if he could take Ethan and me into his unit.

"I want to, but politics, my friend." The tone of his voice did not leave me with much optimism. Araz told me he would be in touch in another two days, which left me and Ethan in limbo. What were we going to do if General Araz couldn't take us? The options weren't very good. There were other Westerners fighting against ISIS with the YPG in Syria, but I wasn't thrilled with that idea. The YPG is a Kurdish militia that is essentially the Syrian branch of the PKK. My experience with the PKK was more than enough to keep me away from the YPG. The Peshmerga referred to the YPG as a bunch of unprofessional monkeys, and I didn't want to associate myself with them. Another option was to join a Christian militia, so that became our Plan B in case things with the Peshmerga and General Araz fell through. I don't consider myself a Christian, but it's a cause I would feel comfortable aligning myself with.

In the meantime we decided not to dwell on the unhappy prospect of being cut out from the Peshmerga. We had just had two amazing days off from duty and there was now no reason why the fun couldn't continue.

THE GIRL FROM REGINA WHO HAD INTRODUCED ME TO CAMPBELL MacDiarmid was in a resort called Lake Dukan, a giant reservoir in the north of Kurdistan, about thirty kilometres from the Iranian border. I called up Lieutenant Ali and bitched to him about being jerked around by General Araz, and then asked if he would drive us to the resort, which he agreed to do. However, it was not Ali who actually picked us up—"I'm busy with paperwork," he said. Rather, it was his personal driver, a corporal in the Peshmerga who couldn't speak a lick of English. Nevertheless, he pulled up in Ali's truck and took us into the mountainous region of northern Kurdistan. The rocky peaks were covered in snow and the air was much colder and fresher here. We passed over small bridges that spanned tiny streams and rivulets and I wondered if people fish in Kurdistan, because the small streams reminded me of the trout creeks back home. I liked the bracing weather in the Kurdish mountains because it reminded me of Canada, though I doubt my Texan friend was feeling the same way.

As it was winter and cold by Kurdish standards, the resort was in its off-season. Rooms were cheaper and there weren't too many guests present. The girl from Regina was gone for the day, but we met up with her friends and some other girls. It was early afternoon and they were already wasted like a troupe of college girls on spring break. Their room was disgusting and filthy, like a bunch of animals had been using it as a pen, and I got a bad feeling about these ladies right away. It took only an hour for things to sour more, as Ethan got into an argument with one of the girls. She was a black, liberal lesbian and it started when she referred to herself as being "African American."

"No, you're not," Ethan corrected her, and technically, he was right. Like all good Texans, Ethan is a strident American patriot and the problem for him was that the girl was not actually an American. "You're not American. You're European, so don't go around saying you are African American. Just say you are black or whatever." *Fuck sakes, Ethan, let it go,* I thought to myself. *I'm trying to get with a girl and you are going to mess this up.*

Anyway, they told us a story of tents catching fire in a refugee camp that they volunteered at. A little boy was killed in the blaze. They were laughing as they told the story.

*All right, that's enough.* We grabbed our shit and left. They were truly a disgusting bunch and I'm ashamed that one of them was Canadian and could be so callous. We got our own room and had a mellow night before heading back to Sulaymaniyah the next day.

# 15.

# BACK TO THE FRONT

**CHRISTMAS EVE 2014**

BACK IN THE DINGY HOTEL ROOM IN SULI, I CONTINUED TO WAIT with Ethan for a call from General Araz, which never came. It was Christmas Eve and a low point for me. The two additional days that Araz had asked for to sort things out had long since come and gone. So I waited, hoping that my phone would light up from his call. I missed my family in Canada and knew that they would all be gathering at my parents' house. I texted with them and knew they missed me too. They had by this point given up on trying to persuade me to come home and instead gave me as much support as they could from halfway around the world.

The lack of communication from General Araz made me think that my mission was over, and it struck with equal measures of anger and disappointment. Sure, I had been in battle and spent time at the front, but I had only been in Kurdistan for a little over a month and it wasn't nearly long enough. If I were to return to

Canada at this point, I would see my mission and myself as a failure even though the reason was largely out of my hands.

Ethan and I had pretty much given up on being accepted back into the Peshmerga when Lieutenant Ali called. It was late at night, but his voice was cheerful, which was a good sign.

"You are good to go," he said. Ali and Araz had talked mere moments before and because the general could not speak much English, he had asked Ali to make the call on his behalf. Ethan and I were pumped on hearing the news.

"Are you driving us to Daquq?" I asked.

"No. Two other Peshmerga will pick you up tomorrow morning, so make sure you have everything ready to go."

*Sweet.* We were going back to the front.

## CHRISTMAS DAY 2014

JUST AS ALI HAD PROMISED, TWO PESHMERGA SOLDIERS ARRIVED at our hotel and we loaded up our gear into the back of their truck. The destination was Daquq, right on the front lines, and the thought of driving with two strangers that close to the enemy was a bit unnerving. For all we knew, these two soldiers were plants and we could find ourselves kidnapped and handed over to the jihadis. In hindsight it seems ridiculous, but when you are in a war zone, your mind dreams up scary scenarios like this. It's probably a primeval defence mechanism to keep us alert. Ethan had the same feeling, though, and the night before we talked about sitting in the back of the truck with concealed knives on us, which we did. Throughout the drive, we didn't talk much to the drivers and they didn't seem overly friendly, which didn't help ease our fears. But sure enough, we reached Daquq safely and disembarked at the base.

We were shown into a foyer outside of General Araz's office, and through the windows we could see him at his desk, which was covered in paperwork, with three Iranian officers sitting across from him. The Shia militias fighting ISIS are funded—and in many cases commanded—by the Iranian army, and so it's a fact of life that Kurdish and Iranian officers liaise with one another. Sometimes it revolves around coordinating military action against ISIS, but most of the time it's about keeping both sides away from each other so that a second war doesn't break out. There is no love between the Kurds and Shia Arabs backed by Iran, but the common enemy has compelled them to work together—or at the very least, not kill each other.

During my stay with General Araz, Ethan and I were forbidden to leave the base and go to Daquq, a city of about 100,000 people, unless accompanied by Araz's personal bodyguards. The reason was the local Shia militias. Keep in mind that these were the same fighters who had happily battled American troops in a long, drawn-out insurgency after the fall of Saddam Hussein. The Shia militias would have thought nothing about kidnapping and killing Ethan and me, or any other Westerner, for that matter. Such was the distrust of the Shia that even Peshmerga soldiers were not allowed to venture into Daquq alone. I remember one time Ethan and one other Peshmerga soldier went into the city to get some smokes and food and as soon as Araz found out, his personal guard flew out of the base in trucks and brought them back to base. The soldier Ethan was with got a severe jacking and from then on we would have to get people to pick us up the things we wanted to buy—mostly food, because we were always starving.

The three Iranians left and we took that as our cue to enter the general's office. He motioned us in and we sat down, with his aide quickly getting us some drinks. Like I said before, the general's English was broken, but we carried on a lighthearted, shooting-the-shit type of conversation for about fifteen minutes, with Araz offering his apologies for keeping us waiting in Sulaymaniyah for so long.

"Not a problem," I said. It *had* been a problem and the wait had stressed me out, but what else could I say to a general?

My Christmas present was an AK-47 from the weapons depot on base. There was no wrapping paper and bow to untie. I checked the gun's firing mechanism and action. Next, we were shown to our quarters, which was a centralized housing unit. This one was fancy, with carpets, windows and a real door—luxury living on the front lines. In fact, this was probably the best-outfitted FOB I had come across in Kurdistan. This particular base garrisoned about a hundred soldiers and served as a headquarters company for Araz and his 9th Brigade. The general was spending his own money to make substantial upgrades, like a new mess hall with tiled floors and decked-out housing units for his men. We learned quickly that he had a generous reputation among his soldiers because he took care of them.

Araz's 9th Brigade was responsible for a large section of the front near Daquq, with multiple bases, but I stayed at the HQ. We shared our housing unit with a lieutenant and got settled into our new routine. We would wake up early, have a breakfast of beans, rice, tomato sauce and flatbread (which was also what we ate for lunch and dinner), and then sit around and wait.

"Hurry up and wait" is a popular expression in the Canadian army, though I've heard soldiers from the American and South African armies use the term too, so maybe it's more widespread than just the frozen north. "Hurry up and wait" basically means that even if you aren't doing anything productive, you have to be ready to move at a moment's notice. That's what it was like on the Daquq front. It's a cliché that warfare is ninety-nine per cent boredom and one percent sheer terror. I was never afraid of being in battle, but I can certainly attest to being bored ninety-nine per cent of the time. But that's just the way it is, in this and any other war throughout history. Even in the First World War, when the Allies and Central Powers clawed at each others' jugulars for four years, it's not like men were going over the top every day. I'm sure it was ninety-nine per cent boredom for those soldiers too.

If my Papa McNicol were still around, I would ask him the same question about the Second World War. Actually, I would ask him a lot of questions about his war. He flew combat missions against the Japanese as part of a British carrier fleet, though from what I've been told he never talked about his combat experience, except with old friends he served with. I guess you can say I come from a family with a history of military service, with my great-grandfather and Papa leading the way in the two world wars. Then there is my uncle Mark Hillier, who served in Bosnia and Afghanistan. We were actually in the PPCLI together and posted at Canadian Forces Base Shilo at the same time.

I REALLY ENJOYED BEING BACK AT THE FRONT, BUT IF I HAD ONE complaint, and it's a small one, it's that I never really knew what would happen from one minute to the next. One moment I would be shooting the shit with Ethan or smoking a hookah with the lieutenant, and the next there would be someone banging on our door, telling us to get ready for a patrol. There was such a communication barrier that we had no warning that we might be called upon to get ready for a mission. Not knowing what the next moment will bring irritates me. I like to have some knowledge and control over what's happening. That's what I hated most about basic training in the Canadian army. It wasn't the runs at 0530 hours, or the endless physical training or lack of sleep, it was the knowledge that at any moment the routine that I thought I was in could be broken.

Araz was a busy general. You have to be when you are responsible for thousands of soldiers and a large stretch of the front. A mistake in the placement of men and supplies could have devastating consequences, and so almost every day we would conduct mounted patrols in Araz's area of operation. We would leave base in the morning in a convoy of ten trucks and be gone for anywhere between one and twelve hours. The convoy was a motley crew consisting mostly of white Toyota trucks, but also a Ford F-350, a Humvee and an SUV that Araz rode in. Except for the Toyotas, everything had previously been owned by the Iraqi army before it fled from Kirkuk. I say without hesitation that the Kurds are putting this material to better use than the Iraqis ever did.

I called these "presence patrols" because the purpose was to let the men on the front lines know that their general was with them. Though the line of defensive berms in the Daquq sector was continuous, they were not fully manned. There simply aren't enough men to defend every foot of trench, and so there were huge gaps in the lines where not a single soldier could be found. To compensate for this weakness, strongpoints were created and spaced at semi-regular intervals throughout the front. A strongpoint was a manmade earthen hill with a command post and garrison on top. The military logic was that if ISIS entered the unmanned sections of the trenches, they would be vulnerable from Kurdish forces that would have the advantage of being on elevated ground. It's a basic maxim of warfare that whoever holds the high ground also holds the tactical advantage. If ISIS did infiltrate the gaps, Kurdish fire would pour into their ranks from multiple directions and angles.

It was at these strongpoints that our convoy would halt. We would all pile out and General Araz would personally inspect the troops and their gear. It was a chance for the officers in charge, usually a captain or lieutenant, to tell the general that they needed more ammunition, weaponry or supplies. But it was also a morale boost for the soldiers to see their general taking a personal interest in their posts. Not that the Peshmerga's morale really needed a shot in the arm; on the contrary, they were well disciplined and had the elusive will to fight that is so apparently absent in the Iraqi national army. Yet it was late December and the soldiers were cold and bored and the presence of a general can do wonders in these circumstances.

These stops were also opportunities to scope out the enemy and see what they were up to. General Araz would always be at the front, observing the jihadi fortifications, numbers, terrain, and so on. He would often personally direct probing fire at the enemy lines to see what we could flush out. During these stops, I would often find an observation point—usually just a gap in the sandbag walls—and peer across no-man's-land into the enemy lines. If the enemy was far enough away I could look on with my scope to get a better view without worrying about cover or a sniper's bullet.

Immediately after the battle of Tal al-Ward, Araz had ordered the construction of what was probably the largest strongpoint in his area of operation. We stopped here to take a look at its progress, which by this point was well under way. Heavy machinery sat idle behind a small mountain of piled earth, stones and rubble. The scale of this artificial hill was impressive; it rose a couple hundred feet from the flat green plains that stretched as far as the eye could see. At the western base of the hill, which faced the enemy, a fifty-metre swath of ground had been cut out from the natural grade of the land. It was like a dry moat from a medieval castle. If ISIS attacked this position, its fighters would have to cross a kilometre of open ground with nothing so much as a shrub to take cover behind, and then plunge straight down into the dry moat. If they were still alive, they would have to actually cross the fifty-metre width of the moat and then begin a ninety-metre climb up the barren face of the rubble-strewn hill—all the while being completely exposed to Kurdish fire. For all intents and purposes, this was a fortress, but Araz wasn't done yet. There were still redoubts, trenches, sandbag walls and concrete bunkers that were in the process of being constructed. Provided his soldiers had enough ammunition and weaponry, not a man could survive trying to take this position.

The only problem was that ISIS was busy doing the exact same thing. In the distance we could see mounds of dirt rising conspicuously from the green plains at regular intervals, as ISIS was making its own strongpoints. Any attacking force from either side would be severely punished in trying to capture ground, and you can see how easily trench warfare becomes stalemated and static. Even in victory, it would cost many lives to cross no-man's-land here.

The Kurds had a truck-mounted DShK machine gun stationed on top of the manmade hill and Araz moved up beside it, his entourage following close behind. Ethan and I were observing the land, looking at the distant strongpoints that we had already visited that day. To the west, the evening sun was beginning to lower over the enemy lines. Araz was pointing at a lone white shack that was sitting in no-man's-land, a little closer to the enemy lines than to our own. It was a decrepit structure that listed to one side in disrepair.

*Crack!* A single round from the DShK shot out towards the listing building. The bullet missed and Araz gave the command to fire again. *Crack!* Another solitary shot roared across the plains, this time hitting a little closer, showering the shack in a spray of parched earth. The DShK can shoot off six hundred fist-sized rounds a minute, but Kurdish ammunition supplies are so low that they cannot spare a burst of fire unless there is a very clear target. Yet this was just probing fire to see if the enemy could be flushed out, and so the ammunition was used sparingly. Before the third shot had fired, a herder and his flock of goats emerged running from the shack and the Kurds held their fire.

The herder was probably supporting ISIS, but he wasn't much of a threat. The PKK I had been with probably would have gunned him down without much thought, but thankfully the Peshmerga were more professional and simply watched as the man ran for all he was worth. Then a truck suddenly peeled off from behind the same building, making a break for the protection of the closest ISIS strongpoint. There was shouting and excitement from the Kurds as the truck sped off over the grassy scrublands, and the DShK gunner didn't wait for an order to pull the cocking hammer back on his weapon. He knew what to do.

*Thump! Thump! Thump! Thump!* The heavy machine gun sprang to life. The truck was fast, but you can't outrun a bullet, and once the gunner had the range the vehicle was torn to pieces. The incoming fire halted and then turned the white truck and its driver into a whirlwind of dust, turf and scrap metal that blasted off in every direction. The stilled heap of wreckage had come to a stop about a kilometre away, well within ISIS territory, and so it was impossible to determine if the occupants were killed. Still, after the dust settled, we couldn't see any movement through our binoculars.

*Unlucky motherfuckers.* General Araz looked pleased with himself for directing the fire that spooked the vehicle, and the rest of the Kurds followed suit with big smiles and happy voices. It was one less enemy vehicle and fighter to worry about. Meanwhile, the goat herder had beaten a hasty retreat. We could see his herd, but it looked as though he had taken shelter behind a fold in the land. I don't blame him. The Kurds wouldn't have shot at him, but under the Caliphate, civilians are killed without regard all the time. Why should the shepherd think the Kurds would act any differently?

Lighting up the truck was the most action I saw between Christmas and New Year's Eve 2014. The Daquq front was relatively quiet, but the Peshmerga we stopped to inspect on further patrols would talk freely about what they had witnessed. There were stories of skirmishes, artillery attacks, mortars, ISIS fighters surrendering themselves and also small bands of refugees crossing into Kurdish territory. The black flags of ISIS were always a familiar sight in the distance and I fantasized about joining a massive attack that would dislodge them from their positions. Then, when enemy fighters were in the open and fleeing from our assault, coalition airplanes could smoke them with high-explosive bombs. But it was a fantasy, at least for now.

I shake my head when I read about politicians and talking heads in the media spouting off against the ineffectiveness of coalition air strikes. In every battle I was in, coalition air power played a major role. After Tal al-Ward, the jihadis were severely punished as they fled back to their own lines. There was another night when everyone in Araz's base was getting spooled up for battle at 0200 hours because a nearby position was under attack. I was sleeping when suddenly there was a loud banging at my door. I stepped into the desert night in my battle gear. The entire headquarters was a hive of activity. Men were starting trucks, soldiers were being mustered into squads and .50-calibre ammo belts were being reloaded under the glare of torches. Everyone was pumped that we were going to fight, but no sooner had our convoy left the base than we were called back. French air strikes had broken up the ISIS attack, meaning we could stand down and go back to bed. My blood was up with the anticipation of battle and it was impossible to get any sleep after that.

Air power alone isn't going to win the war against ISIS, but it's sure as hell going to stop the Kurds from losing it. It was the American bombing campaign that blunted the ISIS blitz in the summer of 2014, and without warplanes destroying tanks and artillery batteries from the air, all of Kurdistan might have been lost.

On our patrols I saw lots of Kurdish 57-millimetre anti-aircraft truck cannons, mortars and rockets, but the ISIS stockpile of weaponry far outclasses what the Kurds can bring into the field. Delivering humanitarian aid is great, but it isn't going to do a damn thing about checking the spread of the Caliphate's black flags. Coalition air power is the one weapons advantage the Kurds have in their war against ISIS and its absence would be devastating for their struggle.

# 16.

# THE ADVENTURES OF CHAI BOY

THE DAYS WITH GENERAL ARAZ TICKED BY, AND DESPITE THE
lack of combat and minimal action with the enemy, I was happy
to be doing what I was doing. The patrols gave me a wider view
of the front, and hanging around General Araz provided me a
glimpse of the overall strategic situation. Though it was quiet at
the moment, Daquq was still an active front and it was only a matter of time before things flared up again.

"Big things are coming," Araz would say. "Big battles soon."
I'm not sure if it's a national trait, but the Kurds seem to have a way
with telling you what you want to hear. Maybe that was just my
experience, but it happened all the time. They knew I wanted at
the enemy, and so every few days there was another big battle just
around the corner. Nevertheless, every time I heard those words I
fought the smile that tried to spread across my face.

Even though we never knew from one minute to the next
when we would be getting spooled up for patrol because of the

lack of communication, Ethan and I found a way to accurately determine if there would be a chance of enemy encounters.

"Chai Boy" was the name Ethan gave to the young corporal who served as General Araz's aide, and if he was present on the patrol it meant that we could relax a little, because there was no way in hell he would be taken anywhere near a serious action. Chai Boy was adept at cleaning ashtrays and fetching soda pops for the general; he was also the most ridiculous-looking Peshmerga I ever saw. Just looking at him cracked Ethan and me up. But it wasn't just us two Westerners who had a good laugh at Chai Boy's expense—the rest of the general's security detail couldn't hold it in, either. Let me explain.

First of all, Chai Boy was a nice guy in person, but his position serving the general, and the menial tasks that go along with that duty, had instilled in him the notion that he somehow had to compensate while on patrol. Thus, he took it upon himself to become the most badass dude to ever wear a uniform.

"Dillon, can you see if my camera is on?" Ethan was asking if I could see the red recording light on his GoPro camera as we sat in the bed of a pickup truck during a mounted patrol. I nodded my head yes. There were three other Kurds with us and to our misfortune, the general's aide was one of them. Ethan took this as an opportunity to film the first of several instalments of *The Adventures of Chai Boy*. Ethan is a switched-on dude, but he also has an awesome sense of humour, which he demonstrated while expertly narrating the impromptu Chai Boy documentary.

While the rest of us were huddled, trying to stay warm in the back of the moving truck with toques and various arid camo–patterned jackets and hoodies covering our freezing bodies, Chai Boy sat on the back of the truck, one leg draped over the hatch like a SWAT team operator ready for action. He was excessively geared up and all his shit looked like it had been dragged from a Tasco catalogue. Ethan spoke into the camera, hilariously itemizing each piece of gear.

"Chai Boy has an airsoft pistol strapped to his thigh, a bundle of plastic zip-tie cuffs dangling from his ass, knee pads on his knees, elbow pads on his ankles, every piece of tactical gear known to man, a fully extended plastic baton strapped to his backpack, ready to go, every morale patch known to man, a rape whistle, padlock, plastic grenade, a broomstick, a flashlight, double mags, a million pieces of rails on his AK–47 that he isn't using for anything . . . did I mention his green laser light? He's using that a lot and he's hanging out of the truck like a goddamn commando."

Ethan took a breath and kept going. "He's also got a night vision mount . . . none of the Kurds on this fucking base has night vision *at all*. I've seen only one set of night vision goggles since I've been in country, so this kid is really just cracking me the fuck up right now."

The two of us were killing ourselves laughing, but the adventures of Chai Boy didn't stop there. Our convoy moved into a town and the traffic brought our pace to a crawl. About a dozen of Araz's security detail got out of their trucks and began walking alongside the convoy. Suddenly Chai Boy sprang into action and sprinted to the head of the detail, zip-tie cuffs flapping about his butt like a beaver tail. The rest of the security team started howling with laughter, which turned into howls of anger. It was night and Chai Boy was shining his green laser pointer at every oncoming truck, whether it was military or civilian. It looked like a *Star Wars* light sabre cutting across the street.

*Fuck, he's going to get himself shot.* Apparently, the Kurds felt the same way. They bundled Chai Boy back into another truck, where he resumed the commando position minus the laser pointer—one leg in the bed, the other leg dangling out the back of the hatch. Part of me felt bad for laughing at the kid's expense because his heart was in the right place, but at the same time, a little comedic relief was necessary. More than anything else, Chai Boy wants to prove himself to his people and I hope he gets that chance. If he does, ISIS should be worried, because from what I've seen there is no better-equipped or gung-ho soldier on the entire front than that young man.

# 17.

# NEW YEAR'S EVE

THE PESHMERGA IS A VOLUNTEER FIGHTING FORCE OF CIVILIAN soldiers. Men are attached to regiments and brigades, they spend anywhere from a week to fifteen days at the front, and then they return home to their families and jobs for a similar amount of time. After a week at the front, General Araz had his driver bring Ethan and me back to the dingy Dindin hotel in Sulaymaniyah and paid for our accommodations. Coincidentally, we arrived on New Year's Eve and it turns out the Kurds celebrate the occasion just like everywhere else in the world. Back home there would be parties, champagne and a countdown to ring in the New Year, and so there was no way we were going to spend the night in our shitty, cold little room. Ethan sprang for a night at the Grand Millennium so that we could bring in the New Year in style. The five-star hotel even had hot water and towels. There was no comparison with the Dindin.

We checked in and had a drink in a quiet lounge on the ground floor. From our table I could see the splendour of the foyer and entrance, the waterfalls outside the glass windows and the immaculately polished tile floors. But there was something else I noticed: a familiar face. A group of five white guys were at the front desk and making their way for the exit. Even though they were wearing civilian clothing, everything about them—their posture, gait and mannerisms—screamed "military" and "special forces." The face I recognized belonged to a guy I served with in the 2nd Battalion, PPCLI. "Grundle" was his nickname and I knew he had gone on to do things with Joint Task Force 2. We weren't close friends, but I knew him well enough to go over and say hello.

"Hey, I'm staying here too. We should meet up later and have a drink." After all, it's not every day you run into an old army comrade in Kurdistan.

Grundle and his friends were not at all thrilled to see me— that much was made clear by the looks on their faces. "Yeah, we'll see . . . I gotta go," he said, and they walked away as briskly as they could.

*Arrogant bastards.* But by and large that's the way of JTF2, especially with the new guys. JTF2, like all special forces, value secrecy and anonymity above all else and even though I was a friendly, I had busted their operational secrecy. Not to mention I was playing in their sandbox. They would have been quite happy to have no other Westerners present in Kurdistan, and this attitude would eventually cause problems for Ethan and me. In the meantime, *screw them.* We were all there for the same cause and purpose.

We took a cab to the fancy Italian restaurant, with sights set on an awesome meal consisting of something other than rice and beans. Yet just as I could spot the JTF2 soldiers out of uniform, two Irish private military contractors spotted Ethan and me and waved us over to their table. They were stationed in the Kurdish capital of Erbil doing VIP security and were fascinated with what we had been up to. They hadn't seen combat, but on the other hand they were making truckloads of money protecting important people. Another guy in his late thirties overheard our conversation and pulled up a chair at our table. He was an Argentine named Maximillano and had previously been in the French Foreign Legion. Now he was in Kurdistan doing what I was doing. In fact, he was stationed at the same train station I had stayed at before going to the front at Rashad. Ethan and I had literally just missed him. We asked about the situation at Rashad and apparently it had been pretty quiet, just as it was when I was there. However, Maximillano was doing really cool shit, including training a sniper team. We exchanged contact information and promised to help each other out if, for whatever reason, things didn't work out in our respective units.

It's funny to think that two Irish contractors, a former Argentine French Foreign Legion soldier, a former marine and a former PPCLI soldier could, by chance, all be sitting around a table in Kurdistan enjoying an Italian meal. But like I've said, it's a strange country that attracts all kinds of people. We finished our drinks and then headed back to the Grand Millennium. I'm not going to say I was drunk, but I would have blown over the legal amount in Canada (it was New Year's Eve, after all).

I saw Grundle and the JTF2 guys drinking in the bar and this time they were a little more talkative. And then I headed off to bed. Ethan and I hung out in Sulaymaniyah for a few more days, checking out coffee shops and the bazaars, but by the time we got the call from Araz's men to get ready, we had seen enough and wanted to get out of the city. The general's motorcade picked us up in front of the Dindin hotel and then sped off to Araz's house in a really nice neighbourhood in an affluent part of the city. Then we headed west, through the mountains and into the flatlands of the front.

# 18.

# BULLET VISION

BACK AT GENERAL ARAZ'S HEADQUARTERS, WE FOUND OUR OLD quarters and fell into the same routine as before—meaning patrols and lots of downtime. I felt like I was wasting away. The diet of beans and rice was taking a toll on my body and I could only guess how much weight and muscle I had lost since being in country. We tried staying fit with some physical training, but I personally found staying fit difficult given the diet I was on. Both Ethan and I wanted to get into some more direct action with the enemy, and we weren't confident that it would happen while stationed in General Araz's front. We didn't know at the time how wrong we were. A battle of epic proportions lay just a few days away and it would test us in ways that we couldn't imagine.

The Peshmerga has a fairly rigid chain of command that any Western soldier would appreciate. There are platoons, companies, regiments and brigades modelled on the NATO standard. The overall command of all Peshmerga units fell under a man named Sheik Jaffer. Nothing of any significance happened in the Peshmerga without Sheik Jaffer's blessing, including the continued presence of Ethan and me.

Maximillano, our Argentine friend, had given me the number of an officer named Akam, who was Sheik Jaffer's right-hand man. Thankfully, he spoke English and I called him to see if there was any chance I could move freely between units, based upon their operational needs. Ideally, Ethan and I would travel to different parts of the country and attach ourselves to units that were in the thick of the fighting. Akam was sympathetic to the request. Apparently, Sheik Jaffer wanted the few Western volunteers to be able to move with more fluidity to areas of the front that were hot, but there was enormous political pressure to keep us contained in the "quiet areas." That's what we had suspected, and it pissed me off. According to Akam, the Canadian and American governments were leaning heavily on the Kurdistan Regional Government to eject us entirely. The last thing the politicians wanted was for either of us to be killed or captured. Also, the military didn't want other Westerners operating in the presence of special forces, due to operational secrecy. Essentially, my own government viewed me as a political liability.

I knew after talking with Akam that I was on borrowed time on my mission in Kurdistan. It was a matter of when, not if, the Canadian government would be able to convince or coerce the KRG into giving me the boot. This belief was strengthened a day later. Ethan and I travelled with General Araz to the K1 military base at Kirkuk for a meeting. On my previous visits to K1, I had been the only Westerner. But upon our arrival, we saw two white guys in civilian clothes tossing a football around. Araz went into his meeting and then we went over to see who these guys were.

They were big dudes, U.S. Army Special Forces—better known as the Green Berets (like Rambo). They were also super-friendly, unlike the Canadian JTF2, and we talked with them for about twenty minutes.

"You guys are badass. If I was out of the military, I'd be doing the same thing," one of them said. We filled them in on what we were doing with Araz, though I suspect they already knew who we were.

"I have to say this," the other man said. "*Some* people don't want you here." He didn't have to elaborate. "Some people" meant the higher-ups in his chain of command. "That being said," he continued, "if you ever need our help, call this number," and he scratched out a phone number on a piece of paper.

"We Americans take care of each other," Ethan said afterwards. It was a shot meant to contrast JTF2's superiority complex with the down-to-earth attitude of the Green Berets. I couldn't argue with him. The Green Berets were solid dudes and it was nice knowing that they had our backs.

**9 JANUARY 2015**
**DAQUQ FRONT**
**0200 HRS**
"FUCK, ETHAN. GET UP, MAN."

Someone was smashing on the door to our quarters with a heavy fist. I rolled on my bed mat and saw that the Texan was already stirring awake from the clamour. The hard knocking stopped and then started again a moment later at the Sea Can next door. I focused my bleary eyes on my watch: it was 0200 hours and I could tell from the sounds outside that the base was alive. For men to be banging on doors, shouting and starting trucks at this hour, it could only mean that something serious was up. And it was.

That very night, ISIS had made a move like George Washington crossing the Delaware, launching an audacious surprise attack against Kurdish forces holding a town called Gwer, about forty kilometres southwest of Erbil. There was a fog covering the river Zab that night, which gave cover to the jihadists as they crossed the water in boats. Like a beast emerging from the mist, ISIS took the Kurds by surprise and inflicted dozens of casualties on them. The entire front blew up that night.

Though the attack on Gwer was over a hundred kilometres to the northwest of my location, the dominos started falling and the quiet of the night fled from the coming battle as the Daquq front mobilized for killing. Like I said before, trench warfare is ninety-nine per cent boredom and one per cent action. This was the one per cent, the moment in time when men prepare themselves for blood and combat, asking themselves if today is their last day. But in the moment, all you can do is get ready and prepare yourself.

Someone banged on our door again and this time one of Araz's men entered. He saw that we were already getting spooled up for action. Combats, boots, body armour, full canteens, warm clothes, AK rifles, rucksacks, TAC vests, magazines holding thirty rounds each.

Through his broken English we came to understand the situation at Gwer. The Kurds had been pushed back by the ISIS attack and they needed our help. The jihadists aren't stupid, and they learned quickly that the threat of air strikes is nullified when there is darkness and thick fog, because the pilots can't mark targets in such weather. During the Second World War, Germany launched its last major offensive in the west in late autumn 1944, using the same considerations—seasonal fog limited the effectiveness of allied air power, giving the Germans a desperate glimmer of hope. In Iraq, when the mist and fog roll in and cover the land, you have to assume ISIS is coming.

I STEPPED OUT INTO THE NIGHT AND SAW TRUCKS BEING FUELLED up and started, weapon belts being loaded, men running and shouting. Ethan and I were ready to go. We helped move some stores and gear into the bed of a truck and then hopped in. I remember all the movement and excitement as our convoy got ready to move. The moments before battle are always like this. Adrenaline starts pumping and you feel in yourself strength as a man and as a warrior. There is no doubting or questioning your purpose in life. You must kill the enemy. *I will kill the enemy.* I can't lie about this: the feeling is intoxicating.

A line of trucks covered with armed men left the base and drove into the winter night. It was cold, and as the vehicles picked up speed the wind bit at our skin. It was nothing like winter in Canada, but I was happy to have my black toque and gloves on. Ethan was well dressed too, but his Texas blood was probably still freezing. I initially thought we would be heading north, to help stabilize the front at Gwer, but our convoy was headed in the wrong direction.

The vehicles halted outside the perimeter of a small fire base near the front lines. In normal times, the small huddle of cement-block guard towers and shipping containers would be garrisoned by maybe two dozen soldiers. Now it was a hub of activity. Araz was using it as a staging area for the units being called up to the front. Convoys of soldiers would arrive from the rear echelon and then be directed to various locations on the front lines. Araz was the maestro, his soldiers the orchestra, and the battle was his theatre. There wasn't a lot of talking with the Peshmerga in our truck, but Ethan and I did the best we could to interact with them using body language and the few spoken words we shared in common. *Fuck, fucking* and *fuckers* were the most common.

I watched as mortars were set up and fired into the distance. The sound of the mortar rounds being fired off was easy on the ears, like a gentle puff. The Katyusha rockets, on the other hand, were chilling. There were several trucks with mounted rocket batteries, and the rounds screeched and howled into the night. I watched as they traced flames through the night sky until they stopped with far-off crashes and explosions. The convoy was parked on a road about fifteen metres outside the fire base perimeter and a mobile rocket battery was immediately behind us. The rockets howled directly over us, and not a man could stop from flinching as they passed over our heads, even though we knew each time when they were coming. Such were the sounds they made, and we felt the air whoosh on our faces and necks.

Our stop at the fire base was longer than I had expected, but General Araz was no doubt busy dispatching the new arrivals to the far-flung stations of his area of operation. When we finally started to roll again, it was on dirt and gravel roads through a deserted landscape, and the pale signs of dawn were just beginning to show on the eastern horizon. Our destination was a small village called Kobani (not to be confused with the Syrian city of the same name). Like most of the villages and towns of the region, there is a Kurdish name and an Arab name for the same place, and the Arabs referred to this settlement as Arabcoy.

The Iraqi Kobani was nothing like the Syrian Kobani. For starters, this was no city and it was far away from the camera crews and journalists of the international media, so you would never hear about it on the six o'clock news. The Iraqi Kobani was a village with homes made of mud and cement blocks. No structure was more than three storeys tall. It was sparsely populated, dirty and run down—in other words, just like all the other little villages and towns that dot the front lines. The general decrepitude of these villages reminds me in many ways of the lawless frontier settlements depicted in Hollywood Westerns, with doors off their hinges, creaking floors and leaking roofs. The only difference was that places like Kobani, Rashad and Tal al-Ward have been like this for hundreds of years and in another hundred years will probably still look the same.

The line of trucks parked behind the village, but ISIS must have seen our arrival because bullets started zipping overhead. Our trenches were two hundred metres beyond the cluster of homes, and the enemy lines were just eight hundred metres past that. I noticed right away that unlike Rashad and Tal al-Ward, the Kurdish works at Kobani were pathetic, and a bad feeling turned in my stomach while looking at them from the back of the truck. The main defensive berm was dangerously low—less than a metre and a half high in some places—and the redoubts and bunkers looked far from impressive. I could see that our trenches were already occupied by the Peshmerga, but it was unmistakably clear that this section of the front had been neglected. Kobani was no strongpoint.

There was no point wasting time and letting the enemy snipers get a range on us. About thirty men unloaded from our convoy and started moving through the twisted and deserted streets of the village. Puddles of dirty water from the winter rains splashed against our ankles, but we were safe while inside the maze of homes. However, the open ground between Kobani and our own trenches was a different matter. Once we cleared the final walls of the village, we would be exposed to jihadi marksmen for two hundred metres before reaching the defensive berm. Front-line trenches are typically accessed by entry points that are concealed from the enemy's line of sight. Unfortunately, we didn't have that luxury at Kobani. Simply reaching the trenches in this sector was almost as risky as being stationed along the sandbag wall.

The command was given and our platoon-sized force stepped into the barren land with the enemy waiting for us. At once, snipers began firing and I heard their bullets landing all around us.

SNIPERS ON BOTH SIDES PRIMARILY CARRY THE DRAGUNOV sniper rifle. Like so many of the instruments of war and death found in Iraq, this rifle is 1960s Soviet vintage and you can usually find it in the same dark corners of the world where you can lay hands on an AK-47. It's not the greatest sniper rifle, but it's very common. The real shortcoming of the Dragunov from my experience is that the optics that come with it are terrible and are only 1x magnification. Don't get me wrong: the Dragunov is a deadly weapon and in the right hands it can be effective, but it's not something Western snipers would go into battle with.

Its effective range is eight hundred metres, meaning that our sprint from the mud huts of Kobani to the Kurdish trenches started outside of the rifle's effective range. Yet the closer we got to our own trenches, the more accurate the enemy fire became. The irony was that increasing my proximity to safety was matched by a greater chance of death from ISIS sniper fire.

I covered the two hundred metres quickly and with panting lungs threw myself against the low berm. Rounds were whizzing all around—not just from Soviet Dragunovs, but AKs, machine guns, recoilless rifles and everything else ISIS had been able to smuggle into the country or pillage from the abandoned Iraqi army depots. The incoming fire as we crossed the field was just the start, and it would last forty-eight hours. It was a slugfest at Kobani, and I was in the middle of it. There's nowhere I would have rather been.

I'm more comfortable with the American-made M16 rifle that I used at Tal al-Ward than I am with the Soviet AK-47. First of all, the M16 is an all-around better rifle, and it's more similar to the C7 that I used in the Canadian army. At Araz's base I had asked to be issued with an M16 but there were none around. The armoury was filled with AKs and there were even a few German-made G36 rifles sprinkled around for good measure, but no M16s. I knew I could kill with the M16 and I had faith in it, but the one drawback is the cleaning. The M16 is more susceptible to jamming and stoppages than the AK-47, especially in dirty, muddy trench warfare conditions that characterize the fight against the Islamic State. At Tal al-Ward, I had to clean my M16 at night for fear of it jamming the next day, but I never had that worry with the AK-47. It's a hardy, durable gun and I came to rely on it a lot over the next two days.

I KEPT TIGHT TO THE BERM, NOT DARING TO MOVE AFTER THE sprint. Ethan was close by with the rest of the Kurds who had survived the run and we looked at each other as if to say "holy shit."

It wouldn't be the last time that we saw this expression on each other. Now that I was at the trenches, the earthen berm seemed even more ridiculously low than it did from the village and the bunkers looked more exposed. It was morning, but the sun was shut out from view by a blanket of grey clouds that drizzled rain. The ground I was crouched in was muddy and damp and soon my feet were cold.

Nobody spoke English, so Ethan and I were essentially on our own. There was no one to give us orders, we had no official duties, and so we operated as freelance soldiers. We moved throughout the trenches and found an observation point that allowed us to get a better sense of our area of operation. Behind us was Kobani and to our front, about eight hundred metres away, were the ISIS lines and another small village. Their flags were drooping in the sodden weather. To our right was a road that in more peaceful times connected the two villages together, yet now it was barricaded, scarred from explosions and heavily mined. On our left was a barren, low-lying ridge. Both the Kurdish and ISIS defensive works were anchored at the base of the ridge and the road, for a total length of slightly less than one kilometre.

As the morning crept by the weather became more miserable, but the fighting intensified. The ISIS lines looked just as hastily constructed as our own, as if both sides had only recently come up with the idea to turn this swath of land into a combat zone. But we had enemy targets to aim at. The jihadis were not as consistently visible as I would have liked, but I saw many more enemy fighters than I did at Rashad. The difference was that the defensive works at Rashad were elaborate and in depth, which basically made the fighters on each side invisible. It was definitely not the case at Kobani and though we could see the enemy, they could also see us.

We moved from the observation point, keeping low the entire time so as not to get shot. We crouched and crawled to various places in the berm and sandbag walls where we could fire some shots at the enemy. Sometimes we fired into the darkened recesses of the enemies' exposed fortifications and other times at individuals who were getting a little too careless. We both managed a few quality attempts, but at this range we could never be sure of kills and hits. This was the way of it, sniping at the enemy and taking chances for a kill in the cold and wet mud.

The two of us scurried down the line like this until we reached a partially constructed concrete bunker that offered enough protection to at least let our guard down a little and stretch our legs. There was already a cluster of Peshmerga here, smoking and trying to ignore the increased tempo of the fighting that now included a lot of machine-gun fire and recoilless rifles. A recoilless rifle is another way of saying "shoulder-mounted rocket launcher," and when a shell exploded directly opposite the berm that covered our bunker, it scared the shit out of us. This was the type of weapon that messed up our LAVs (light armoured vehicles) in Afghanistan. The explosion felt massive because it was only a metre and a half away, but our lives were saved by the wall of dirt that we had our backs to. Smoke trailed up from the impact. *We are in the shit.*

It was a close call, but others weren't that lucky. Mere moments later I saw a man get shot in the head. I was looking down the line when I noticed a Peshmerga soldier rise from the protective shadow of the berm and then start casually walking away from the front. I have no idea what he was doing or where he was going, but it was a fatal mistake. It's very easy to misjudge the line of sight that the enemy has, because the terrain rises and falls, just as the height of the defensive berm ebbs and flows. Not to mention, there are a series of angles and multiple directions that you have to account for. In a word, it's impossible to know with one hundred per cent certainty the enemy's line of sight. So the only way to keep safe in the trenches is to keep down.

The Kurdish soldier's head snapped back from the enemy bullet. Two Kurds rushed to pull their comrade to safety, but it was no use. He was dead before he hit the ground. There are degrees of danger in warfare. The man may have been careless or even foolish for standing up where he did, but it was also a lucky shot. Somewhere there was an ISIS sniper laughing and gloating, but we would make the bastards pay.

**1030 HRS**

BY MID-MORNING ALL OF ARAZ'S MEN WHOM WE HAD ARRIVED with had gone. Ethan and I were the only ones left. They didn't tell us that they were leaving; they just packed up and left. We were alone with this new unit of unfamiliar faces. In the bunker, I could see that there was not one dry eye or cheek on any of the men. Not just from the man's death, but for all the others who had so far been killed. The place was a meat grinder.

One of the Kurds next to us had a Dragunov sniper rifle and scope. He wasn't using it and Ethan began using some hand gestures to initiate a temporary trade—his AK for the man's sniper rifle. The Kurd agreed. Most of them thought we were either special forces or spotters for air strikes, and so they didn't ask many questions of us. Not that they spoke English anyway, but it also made them more amenable to trading weapons.

We left the bunker and resumed where we had left off, creeping along the trenches, looking for discreet openings in the sandbag walls and berms where we could get a fix on the enemy. When we found a suitable location we would set up and look for a target. If there were no targets we would train our scopes on an exposed space or area of the enemy lines and then wait for movement.

Ethan was the one who started with the Dragunov first and he manoeuvred into a comfortable position. It was a little more exposed than we wanted, but it offered a pretty good line of sight over the enemy trench. With his one open eye focused through the scope, Ethan lay still and I stretched myself down on the muddy ground beside him. Ethan's job was to stay focused, shoot and kill, while mine was to cover the wide angles and spot for him. The number-one rule of sniping is that you never telescope your bar- rel. In other words, you want to set up so that your barrel doesn't protrude from the cover you're using. Most of the time, our cover was a sandbag wall that had one sandbag removed. These gaps in the wall created spaces big enough to shoot through, sort of like loopholes in old military forts. That was most of the time. As I said before, when we first set up with the Dragunov, we sacrificed cover and protection in exchange for a better line of sight over the enemy works. We almost paid the price for our impudence.

Ethan fired a few inconclusive shots and I continued spotting targets using the clock-ray method—"Twelve o'clock to that con- crete bunker. Two fingers left." Ethan would zero in on the target, which was usually in the form of a flashing enemy rifle muzzle.

But the ISIS snipers were playing the same game and they were dialled into our exposed position. The air was constantly humming with the sounds of incoming fire, like a swarm of angry hornets, but one well-placed shot is better than a spray of ill-aimed continuous fire. Among the vast quantity of high-velocity lead being thrown about, there was one particular bullet that nearly ended this story.

From somewhere in the enemy trenches, or perhaps from a building in the village, a solitary bullet was loosed against me. And I saw it coming. The glint and sheen of the round caught my eye and mesmerized me as it raced across no-man's-land, directly towards me. It was like a split second and an eternity all at once. Life and time became very real when it slammed into the two-foot space between my face and Ethan's. Mud spewed up from the impact and we looked at each other with wild eyes.

"Fuck, man! That was for us."

"Holy shit!"

We slunk behind the berm and hugged the earthen wall tight and then laughed. Having a bullet miss your face by inches isn't funny, but the laughter was an instinctual and emotional release from the trauma that comes from knowing you could easily have been killed. I don't know whether the bullet was intended for me or Ethan (though the bullet made impact a little closer to Ethan's head than mine), but the jihadi knew what he was doing.

We moved on to another position, this time taking pains to properly conceal ourselves. Ethan passed the Dragunov over and it was my turn to shoot. On my watch, some ISIS fighters actually came into view, but I was too slow. It happened again, and this time I squeezed a round off. There was no way of knowing if I got him, but at the very least it would have made him and his friends think.

There were other locations that we set up in and we continued sniping with the Dragunov until our ammunition was nearly spent. There was death on both sides of no-man's-land; you knew it right away when the swirling voices of battle would change for a brief moment and a section of the line would go quiet as men retrieved wounded or dead comrades. The telltale signs of death appeared often on this day.

## 1300 HRS

ALMOST AS IF BY AGREEMENT, THE GUNFIRE ON BOTH SIDES slackened. It didn't disappear entirely, but men have to eat and this was as good a time as any to put down rifles and use fingers for spoons instead of pulling triggers. Cups of rice were passed around sometime that afternoon and I hungrily devoured that unsatisfying meal until the vessel was clean. There had been no word from Araz or any of his men since they left earlier in the morning and we figured the general must be inspecting the other parts of his area of operation. It made sense because the ISIS attack on Gwer had unleashed a firestorm across the entire front. Gwer was only the first domino to fall and everywhere in a line from Mosul in the north to Daquq in the south, the Kurds and ISIS were attacking and counterattacking. The entire front was alive and from multiple directions we could hear the concussion of heavy artillery drumming in the distance.

Everywhere we went, Kurds serving in the Peshmerga greeted us enthusiastically and wanted pictures. During the lull in the fighting, Ethan and I posed for a few shots with some of the Kurdish soldiers who saw us as a novelty. We were always viewed with a curiosity that comes from being the only white guys on the front lines. Through hand signals and very rough English, they asked if we were forward air controllers calling in air strikes, but we shook our heads and said the word *volunteer*, even though they had no idea what that meant.

The lull lasted for twenty or thirty minutes and then the gunfire gradually returned to its baseline intensity. After being awake since 0200 hours and being under fire for hours, I was beginning to feel tired, wet and cold. Everyone was, but that didn't mean the fighting could stop. In fact it wasn't anywhere near over.

Reinforcements in the form of my "friends" in the PKK showed up. I noticed their distinct uniforms sprinkled among the Peshmerga and then saw two women in the trenches. I recognized them as being from PKK Ali's command. They were grinning at me with big smiles, apparently happy to see me. For as much mutual distrust as we held for each other, there was still a respect that comes from entering battle together and they had not forgotten what I did for Brothahan. Their base wasn't too far from Kobani and, like good allies, they had driven to the sounds of the guns.

Tal al-Ward was the only time that I saw the PKK and the Peshmerga working together. By and large they do their own thing and if cooperation does occur, it's more likely to be corollary and incidental than deliberate. There is little on-the-ground coordination and planning between the two forces. The Peshmerga is Kurdistan's official army, yet many of its soldiers look upon the PKK as this awesome, semi-mystical fighting force. Maybe it's because the PKK has been active in combat for so long, launching guerilla raids into Iran and Turkey from its mountain refuges. Its goal is to create a communist Kurdistan that encompasses the regions of Iraq, Turkey, Syria and Iran, and it has been at it for some time. However, with the advance of ISIS, the PKK has wisely turned its attention towards halting the savages at the gates, rather than picking fights with stronger neighbours.

The PKK also has a robust propaganda machine that churns out stories of victory and heroism against great odds. When I was with PKK Ali's men, they told me a story of one hundred PKK killing fourteen hundred Iranian guards in a mountain ambush. I doubt that happened, but there are so many stories of the PKK's exploits that it's no wonder soldiers in the Peshmerga look up to them.

I won't hide my disdain for the PKK, but to give credit where it's due, it might be a decent guerilla force. PKK fighters have a unique way of arriving and disappearing from the battlefield. They can be elusive and obviously have some training in guerilla tactics, but the problem is that this is not a guerilla war. It's trench warfare, the furthest thing from the hit-and-run style of combat that PKK fighters are trained for. The reality is that it was the Peshmerga that checked the ISIS advance at Kurdistan's border, not the PKK.

## 1600 HRS

THE BODY HAS A WAY OF IGNORING PAIN AND FATIGUE IN COMBAT, courtesy of the adrenaline that starts pumping through your veins. It also brings on a sense of hyperalertness, which is the way it has to be; otherwise you'll lose focus, make mistakes and end up dead very quickly. However, there is a breaking point. I wasn't there yet, but I was starting to feel the effects of running on a couple hours of sleep and although I was holding up well enough, I knew I had to eventually rejuvenate myself. There were a couple of bunkers where men could duck out for an hour or two and, if not quite sleep, at least rest their eyes. This is where Ethan and I made our way to.

The bunker, if you could call it that, was the most ridiculous I have ever seen. It was a huge concrete cylinder, like a culvert, that had been incorporated into the berm-and-trench system. Yet safety inside its rounded walls was just an illusion because both of its ends were left uncovered. There was an opening on the Kurdish side of the berm, but you had to crawl in because the opposite end of the cylinder protruded towards the ISIS lines and was only partially covered. A wall of sandbags rose from this opening, but it stopped about two-thirds of the way up, presumably to allow a defender to fire at the enemy. The decision to leave an opening of this size in a bunker, completely exposed to enemy fire, is ludicrous, but that's the way it was.

It was no surprise that ISIS snipers were dialled into this gap between the sandbag wall and the rim of the concrete cylinder, so Ethan and I kept low, very low. I can't believe we even tried to sleep in this place. Numerous bullets were thudding against the sandbags that covered the opening and some were even sailing right through the bunker itself. To say it was unnerving to hear the bullets peppering the bunker would be an understatement; after all, we were putting our faith in a few rows of sandbags. Yet so long as the enemy bullets didn't enter the bunker and then make a sudden ninety-degree turn at the wrong moment, we were safe. Sleep was impossible in these circumstances, so the best we could do was lie down and rest our eyes for a while. It was better than nothing, and I might have even dozed off for a few minutes. Regardless, when I shimmied out of the concrete tunnel I felt a little fresher than when I crawled in.

"YOU GUYS ARE DOING IT WRONG," I TOLD A GROUP OF MEN HUDdled around one of the general-purpose machine guns (GPMGs) available to us. It was a Soviet-made PK machine gun and, like the omnipresent AK-47, this weapon was the child of Mikhail

Kalashnikov. The PK is a belt-fed GPMG mounted on a bipod and is used as a platoon support weapon. There were a few of these Soviet-made guns dispersed along the line, and Ethan and I could see that the Kurds were using them all wrong.

Soldiers in the Canadian army are taught the theory of machine-gun fire, starting in soldier qualification and getting more in depth as your career advances. I could talk about the "beaten zone" and "cone of fire," but the basic thing to know is that a machine gun isn't a sniper rifle. Rather, it's an area weapon and not designed for precision accuracy. I was incredulous watching the Kurds operate the machine gun. They fired single rounds at the enemy when they really should have been firing bursts. Ethan had been trained in the same machine-gun theory as I had, and we tried explaining to the Kurds that they should fire repeatedly in three- and five-second bursts. They either didn't understand or thought they knew best.

Ethan took control of the gun and demonstrated its proper usage, training the barrel on an enemy position and letting loose. *Three.* Pause. *Five.* Pause. *Three.* Pause. *Five.* Pause. He counted the seconds while pressing down on the trigger, but the Kurds were having none of it. The maddening part was that they would fire their rifles like machine guns and their machine guns like rifles, the opposite of what they should have been doing. It's examples like this that show that, even though the Peshmerga is the best military organization in the region, it still needs lots of training and help.

"Fuck, guys. You don't know what you are doing." But it was their weapon and we sat back and watched their ineffectual fire.

# 19.

# A CLOSE CALL

**9 JANUARY 2015**
**1700 HRS**
IT'S A NORMAL BODILY REACTION TO WANT TO PISS RIGHT BEFORE
you go into battle. It's the result of nerves acting up. At Tal al-Ward
I walked into a field, unzipped my pants and took a leak. The
Kurds were laughing when I got back.

"We don't pee standing up," one of them said. When Kurds
have to urinate, they crouch. Some Westerners arrive in foreign
lands and can't wait to start jettisoning their culture and adopting
the norms of their new surroundings. I saw that a lot in Kurdistan,
especially among the liberal aid workers. Yet aside from wearing a
black-and-white checkered scarf around my neck on some occasions, I went out of my way to do things the Western way. I sure as
hell wasn't going to crouch when I pissed.

But I needed to go. Badly.

I left the fortified concrete and sandbag redoubt that I was
in and headed for the communal latrines. There were designated

washroom areas about fifty metres to the rear of the trenches and they were, as you can imagine, the foulest things I have ever crossed. Centralized housing units were commonly converted into sleeping quarters along the front, but at Kobani they were used as latrines. The inside of the containers was separated into several stalls with holes cut out of the floors. Every day, hundreds of soldiers crouched over these holes to piss and shit and they were just Godawful messes. Of course, there was no toilet paper either, which made matters worse. Instead, each stall had a small pipe sticking out from the wall, which was connected to a water silo outside. With a turn of a red lever, water would gush out of the pipe and you would use this in combination with your hand to wipe your ass. It's not the most hygienic way of doing things. Thankfully, it was winter and not summer; otherwise it would have been hard not to puke from the odour. I had been holding it in too long and my bladder was happy to be evacuated. I aimed into the circular hole cut from the floor and looked up to the ceiling with a sigh of relief. Apparently, the latrines were no sanctuary: the top of the container was riddled with bullet holes. There were no safe places at Kobani.

I couldn't wait to step out from the container and once outside I walked briskly, trying to put the nauseous odours behind me. My head was ducked and shoulders stooped as I walked back to the bunker, but this was no stroll in the park. It was my brush with death.

*Fuck!* Bullets began whooshing immediately in front of my face. I could feel the rounds ripping by, compressing the air onto my skin, and I hit the ground just as more bullets zipped overhead. The bunker wasn't too far and I began crawling on my belly through the mud. There was lots of incoming lead in the air, but none directly over me anymore, so I rose gently to my feet and then ran awkwardly with my torso bent at a ninety-degree angle to keep low.

"What the fuck happened to you?" Ethan asked as I re-entered the bunker. Apparently, I didn't look so great after my second near-death experience.

"Don't go to the washroom. I almost got shot." Those were not random bullets from a random ISIS fighter. Some jihadi sniper had me in his sights, and the knowledge sent a chill up my spine. Luckily for me, I was walking sideways and was a moving target, meaning that the sniper had to lead me. In other words, the jihadi would have had his scope aimed just in front of me, so that I would walk into the bullets. But he timed it wrong. Barely. And that's the only reason why I am still alive.

On the front lines, the difference between life and death is sometimes measured in inches. Had I been one pace ahead, I would have been killed. Had the wind been a little different, I would have been killed. Had the sniper breathed properly on the shot, I would have been killed. There are so many variables that I wonder if God was with me. Or maybe I was just lucky?

I let my rifle drop to the ground and took a seat in the cramped bunker. I was almost killed at Tal al-Ward; the enemy bullets at that fight had kicked up dirt inches away from my head. Now this. These bullets were even closer; I saw the blur as they passed in front of my eyes. In the heat of combat, you forget that you can be killed at any moment, but I knew I wasn't invincible. With the sounds of enemy fire thudding against the sandbags, I wondered how much more luck I had left, if any, and I started playing the odds in my head.

For the sake of argument, I figured there was a five per cent chance of getting killed or wounded in any battle. Does that fatality percentage stay the same with each subsequent battle, or does it increase? I came to the conclusion that the chance of getting hit must go up with each battle. The odds aren't independent of previous events; otherwise, I could flip a coin a hundred times and never be surprised if it landed on tails a hundred times. If I was right about this, it meant my chances of being killed increased with every battle that I was in. My God, this thought experiment was getting too mathematical and philosophical, but it made me question a lot of things.

"Do you want to get some more of these fucks?" Ethan asked, and I nodded my head.

"Goddamn right I do."

I wanted to make them pay, not for my near death, but for every single innocent person who had been killed, tortured and raped under their black flags. That's why I was here. I felt angry now, but I would be more cautious. The lesson to stay low had been reinforced.

We borrowed Dragunovs and slinked out of the bunker, crawling to a firing position we had been at before. A shower of lead was still passing overhead, as it had all day, meaning the enemy was active and targets might present themselves. I was in a sick position that gave me a rather wide line of sight on the enemy works. My barrel was pointing still at the opposing lines and I waited, looking for muzzle flashes in the falling light. There were many to choose from and I scoped out the best target. There was flashing coming directly to my front and I waited, letting the enemy combatant fire a few bursts so that he would get comfortable and maybe careless. The flashing muzzle appeared again and again at regular intervals and then, with my barrel calm and rigid, my scope zeroed in, I let loose with my fire. Looking through my scope, I could see that the flashing muzzle had disappeared. Not only that, but the section of the enemy front went quiet for a moment and I fought a grin, knowing what that meant. That was payback. *That was justice, you bastard.*

## 1900 HRS

GENERAL ARAZ AND HIS PERSONAL DETAIL RETURNED TO KOBANI at dusk. Sure enough, they had been a travelling roadshow, visiting the many hotspots encompassed by his area of operation, but they hadn't forgotten about Ethan and me after all. The shooting, both from us and from ISIS, had slackened considerably and while Araz talked to the officer in charge of these trenches, we said some goodbyes and then loaded up into a waiting truck. I was exhausted and starving all at once. After Tal al-Ward, I rode a high for a week, but continuous combat for an entire day in cold, wet weather, combined with virtually no sleep, had left me feeling numb and worn down. I closed my eyes and didn't even care where we were heading.

The ride back to the fire base from which we had started out earlier that morning wasn't long, but I caught a few minutes of sleep through the bumps in the dirt road. That would be all that I would get, because we were staying here for the night. The fire base was still active with soldiers coming and going, but the rockets and mortars had gone silent for the night. We ate some beans with rice and bread and took shifts guarding the perimeter. I doubt I could have gotten much sleep anyway, because air strikes were lighting up the night. Fierce explosions were rocking the jihadi positions up and down the lines throughout the darkened hours. The eruptions of flame and fire would momentarily turn night into day. The enemy was being punished severely from above.

THERE ARE SO MANY STRANGE COINCIDENCES IN WAR. I'VE written about a few chance encounters, like meeting the girl from my hometown and running into Grundle in the lobby of the Grand Millennial. Yet as I listened to the detonations and the aircraft flying overhead that night, I thought of another coincidence and how strange it was that while I was fighting ISIS on the ground, a family friend was fighting them from above.

I'll call him Tom Collins because he's active-duty air force and his chain of command won't allow his real name to be used. He is a friend of my older brother and he grew up just a few doors down from where I grew up in Carleton Place, Ontario. He joined the air force after college and was part of an air crew doing surveillance and marking targets from above. What are the chances of two neighbours from small-town Ontario fighting the same enemy in Iraq? Maybe there's something in Carleton Place's water supply. I hoped to hell that he and the rest of the Canadian contingent flying missions over the Islamic State were marking lots of enemy positions. Judging from the continuous aerial bombardment that night, I think they were.

There was a Kurd who could speak very good English and he had been able to hack into the enemy ICOMMS frequency. A group of men were now huddled around his radio, listening to the ISIS chatter in Arabic. Ethan and I joined the group after a shift on the perimeter and took seats on the ground beside the English speaker.

"What are they saying?"

The enemy words had to be translated from Arabic to Kurdish and then English for us. "They are getting hit hard. Many deaths from the bombs," the man said. We smoked cigarettes and listened silently in the night to the Arabic dialogue. It meant nothing to me, but several of the Kurds could understand. "At least thirty have been killed since the bombing started," the man said after a pause. "Many more wounded." There was excitement at the news. *Shhh!* He rose his hand for quiet. "Also, they say a white jihadi was killed today." *No fucking way.*

*Boom!* Another bomb detonated on the enemy lines to our front and shook the ground. Araz was on his cellphone all night to the Peshmerga command centre in Erbil, giving locations for air strikes, and he looked pleased with the latest explosion.

"What else?"

The man shook his head. "Not much else. They are being killed and taking cover. They won't attack us tonight."

Aircraft kept roaring overhead in continuous sorties and the bombs kept falling. There was no sleep, but my role in the day's fighting was over.

THOUGH THE INITIAL ISIS ASSAULT ON THE TOWN OF GWER WAS successful in taking the Kurds by surprise, Peshmerga reinforcements were able to contain the breach. After hours of intense fighting and coalition air strikes, the jihadis were driven out of the town and back across the river Zab. Their corpses littered the streets and buildings of the strategic settlement, and the bloated bodies of those drowned in the retreat were found washed up on shore afterwards. The fighting that raged up and down the lines at places like Kobani diverted and pinned down ISIS reinforcements, which could have tipped the battle in their favour. It was a Kurdish victory, but one that came at a price. Many Peshmerga were killed in the initial surprise, with still more killed in the diversionary attacks that followed afterwards. Yet the integrity of the front was maintained and when the sun rose over the winter landscape the next day, it was undeniable that ISIS had suffered a terrible defeat.

## 10 JANUARY 2015
## DAQUQ FRONT

A DAY AFTER THE PREVIOUS DAY'S FIGHTING WE WERE SPENT, both mentally and physically. The lack of sleep for two nights and the continuous fighting had left me exhausted. I felt like a zombie and my head ached from the toll that that much stress takes. The previous day's fighting and the air strikes that followed had taken the fight out of ISIS, and the front had finally gone silent. Soon we would go back to Araz's headquarters, but first we went on one more patrol, stopping at hilltop strongpoints and inspecting the fortifications. Most of these stops were easily forgettable, but there was one stop on our route that shook me up.

Our convoy stopped behind a manmade hill and we began trudging up the steps that had been cut into the pile of dirt. We weren't moving quickly and when I got to the top I lit a cigarette and drew deeply. The weather was bracing atop the strongpoint and the green plains spread out before us. ISIS was well over a kilometre away, too far to be of much worry, or so we thought.

Araz and the rest of the men looked across no-man's-land through binoculars and scopes, but the only signs of the enemy were their flags in the distance. That was fine; nobody wanted to fight today anyway. We were played out.

And apparently we had overstayed our welcome.

I heard a boom very far off, followed by a howling screech before the top of the hill blew up in an explosion of earth and fire. Artillery fire! I felt the earth shake and the blast pulsate through my body. The enemy round landed about fifty metres from where I stood, but luckily no one was injured. We didn't wait for the second round to come; we darted back to the sheltered side of the hill. Without a target, the ISIS artillery went back to sleep, but Araz was on his phone, calling it in. Chances are the heavy gun was well hidden—in a village with lots of civilians around, no doubt—but if coalition planes knew what they were looking for and the approximate location, maybe they could take it out. Perhaps it would even be my childhood neighbour who would do the spotting. Probably not, but you wonder about these things.

I kept pace with the online media from Canada, especially the stories about Canadian air strikes on ISIS positions, but one thing I read over and over again was the apparent lack of targets. When I read things like this, I would always shake my head because there are plenty of ISIS targets. Either our guys aren't looking hard enough or there are political directives to avoid collateral damage at all cost. The reality is that an artillery piece in ISIS hands is going to cause casualties, one way or the other. If left alone, it will be used to kill Kurds. If taken out by an air strike, civilians might die. Either way, people will die.

Despite the previous day's battles and air strikes, the incoming fire proved that the enemy still had some bite, and our convoy left, not wanting to give ISIS additional target practice. We were on our way back to Araz's headquarters and I drifted off to sleep in the back of the truck with thoughts of war on my mind.

# 20.

# OUT OF GAS

13 JANUARY 2015
GENERAL ARAZ'S HEADQUARTERS
SLEEP WAS MY ONLY PRIORITY WHEN I GOT BACK TO ARAZ'S headquarters. As soon as the trucks stopped and the gear was unloaded, I booked it for my quarters. Eating, drinking, women and war: none of that mattered in the least. All I needed and wanted was sleep, and mercifully I was allowed to pass out on my bedroll. It was the kind of sleep where your dreams are weird and vivid and you wake up confused and have no idea where you are. So much had happened in the days prior that my mind was having a hard time piecing it all together and making sense of it. But it all came back as soon as I saw my gun lying next to me and the hookah pipe sitting on our small table. I had been out of it for a long while, but I felt refreshed and alive again when I came to.

For a few days after the battle, I got back into the normal base routine—eating, sleeping, even working out a little bit with a dip bar and resistance cables. There were some small patrols thrown in as well to make sure we didn't get overly comfortable, but they were short and the front had been quiet since the Gwer offensives had ended. As far as I know, not much territory, if any, had changed hands, so it was situation normal on the Caliphate–Kurdish border. Yet as much as things had stayed the same on the front lines, things were changing in the rear echelons where I was.

When my mission began, I harboured the hope that I would be the first among many Western volunteers who would eventually arrive in Kurdistan. The dream had been a platoon-sized force at the very least, comprised of Western volunteers who were trained and ready for battle. Of course, this never materialized. Instead of being a trailblazer, I was a lone white guy in a foreign land. Ethan's arrival made it two white men in a strange land, but this was a far cry from the lofty ambitions I had planned with Lieutenant Ali. By January—hell, by mid-December even—it was clear that a Western-trained and professional force operating in Iraq just wasn't going to materialize. By and large, the professional soldiers had stayed home and the few Westerners who did arrive to fight ISIS had gone to Syria to join the YPG.

Syria was the perfect place for untrained and untested Western thrillseekers who wanted a piece of the action against ISIS. The YPG in Syria will hand a gun to anybody who shows up, because there are no standards. And when you have no standards, you draw the wrong kinds of people. I salute these people for putting their lives on the line for a noble cause, yet I'm not going to pretend that they were a professional force, and I know firsthand what ill-disciplined militias in Iraq and Syria are capable of. I have a hard enough time sleeping at night because of the atrocities I saw while attached to the PKK. I don't have to imagine the heinous shit that fighters alongside the YPG have to live with.

# 21.

# NEW ARRIVALS

A FEW DAYS AFTER THE FIGHT AT KOBANI, A MOTLEY CREW OF five Westerners arrived at General Araz's headquarters. You would think that I would be happy to see some fellow Westerners on base, but it was quite the opposite. I recognized James and Juan the Mexican from the Peshmerga base in Sulaymaniyah, but there were three others who raised my suspicions just by their very appearance. If you have ever served in the military, you can easily spot an ex-serviceman by the way they walk, talk and carry themselves. James and Juan had it, but the other three were unquestionably poseurs.

James and Juan came over to say hello and I was genuinely happy to see them, but I had a bad feeling about their companions. There was Sam, a black guy wearing white basketball shoes, blue jeans and a white shirt. He openly admitted to having no military experience, but his heart was in the right place. He was woefully unprepared for life at the front, but at least he didn't try to bullshit his way around anything, unlike the next two, whom I had the displeasure of meeting.

The weirdest guy was named Mickey. One look at his face and garb told me everything I needed to know about him. He claimed to have served in the French Foreign Legion, a claim I disputed right away as being bullshit. He had a full black-and-white skeleton bandana around his neck and when he spoke, I could see that he had his canine teeth elongated into fangs. I also found out a little later that he was also a registered sex offender in Colorado. On his camo vest was a Velcro name tag that read "Necromancer," a moniker he had given himself to flatter his own fantasies. To say that Mickey was a fucked-up individual would be a shameful understatement.

The leader of this gang of misfits and malcontents was called Arman, a German citizen of Kurdish descent. He was also a member of the Median Empire, a European biker gang made up of guys from the Kurdish diaspora. No serious military organization would ever have taken his fat biker ass into its ranks, yet here he was, supposedly in charge of this crew.

Ethan and I shot some conspicuous looks at each other throughout our first meeting with the new arrivals. They were everything you wouldn't want in the man next to you in battle.

"Did you get your fangs done before or after the French Foreign Legion?" I wanted to let this Mickey guy know that I thought he was an idiot.

"After."

"Wait. You are telling me that you got your teeth made into fangs in your thirties?"

"Yeah. I think they look cool," he answered.

"Right. They go really well with your name tag." I just shook my head and looked to James as if to say, "Why the hell are you with these guys?" We found out later that night. In the meantime,

Ethan and I decided to keep our distance from the new arrivals, at least until we learned more about them.

James came over to our quarters later that evening after dinner. We smoked a hookah as he told us what was up. It had been over a month since we had seen him and Juan back in Sulaymaniyah and we filled him in on what we had been doing with Araz, including the fighting at Rashad and Kobani.

But I had to ask him what the hell he was doing with these guys.

James wasn't the most solid dude I have ever met—he had his problems and issues like we all do—but at least he had actually spent time in the American army. Had he been attached to me and Ethan for the last month, he would have been in a better way. Instead, the weeks with Arman and his current comrades had done him no good.

"Fuck, guys, I should have come with you," he said. "Arman, Mickey and Sam have been confined to the Suli base since December. Juan and I should have left them and joined you." He explained the situation in more detail as our room filled up with hookah smoke. Mickey and Sam had come in contact with Arman in much the same way that I had come into contact with Lieutenant Ali. The difference was that Ali was an officer in the Peshmerga and Arman was a biker from Germany. But he had fed Mickey and Sam a bunch of bullshit that he had everything organized for their arrival in Kurdistan. No doubt Arman had expected the red carpet to be rolled out for him and his Western gang, but instead the Peshmerga had detained them at the base in Sulaymaniyah. They were essentially under lockdown and not allowed to leave the base. Nobody trusted them, and for good reason, and so while Ethan and I had been rolling with Araz since our last meeting, James and Juan had been stuck waiting on the three poseurs. At least James and Juan could go into Sulaymaniyah if they wanted to, a luxury Arman and the others weren't afforded.

However, word had gotten to Arman that Araz was accepting Western volunteers and with that knowledge he was able to pull the right strings, talk to the right people, and so here they were. There were other things too, like the group being divided between James and Juan against Arman and Mickey. Sam was somewhere in the middle, too unsure of himself to take sides. This was when James told us about Mickey's status as a sex offender. He looked capable of all sorts of heinous crimes. His seedy background was exposed on the Internet.

"They're losers, James," we said, and he nodded his head in quiet agreement before leaving.

When you are a minority in a foreign land, you try to be on your best behaviour, because whether it's fair or not, you are a representative of your people. This is a truism magnified by a factor of ten when you are with a foreign army and wearing a uniform. Ethan and I were well liked and respected because we did our duty and could be relied upon, and so a day never passed when we weren't invited to eat, smoke and hang out with the various Peshmerga soldiers on base. But Arman's gang never got the message and I worried that their unprofessionalism would reflect badly on Ethan and me, so we did our best to avoid them as much as possible. But that's easier said than done on a small base.

Arman tried getting weapons issued to his gang, but the Peshmerga refused, giving some lame excuse. The truth was that they weren't trusted. Arman was pissed and started marching his fat ass over to us.

"Tell them we are cool and that we need guns."

"I don't speak Kurdish. Can't help you there," I said and he stormed off in a huff.

Over the next couple of days we saw more dissension among the gang of five. James and Arman approached Ethan and me at different times, trying to get us to side with them over differences of opinion on inane things, but it was all drama and we refused to get involved.

Ethan and I sat down one evening for dinner after an uneventful patrol and soon enough the gang of five appeared and started talking about this secret mission they were prepping for. Apparently, they were going to be helicoptered onto Mount Sinjar, west of Mosul, and inserted behind enemy lines. "We are going to gather some intel and then fight our way out," one of them said.

"How are you getting the helicopter?"

"I'm arranging that," Arman answered. *Sure you are, you fat bastard.*

"How are you going to get resupplied with water and ammunition?"

"There won't be any resupply," James spoke up.

"And we don't care if we die," Juan added.

"Well, that's stupid." There wasn't anything else to say. These guys were like a bunch of delusional clowns. Each one of them seemed to have a death wish and was running from something— James from a marriage and unwanted kids, Juan from a domestic and weapons charges, Mickey from a sex offence and God only knows what else. Arman was a hero in his own mind.

Lord Wellington referred to the common British soldier as the "scum of the earth," but that was nothing compared to the gang of five. Sam was the only one I couldn't figure out, but in my mind he was guilty of something by association. These weren't the kind of guys I wanted to fight beside. A single man with a death wish is dangerous mostly to himself. Five men with death wishes are dangerous to everyone around them.

The next day, Arman got his way and the Peshmerga issued the new arrivals with weapons. Juan and James knew how to use their AKs, while Arman and Mickey would figure theirs out. Sam, on the other hand, was given a PKC machine gun.

"What the fuck?" Ethan and I said together as we watched the distribution. *What the hell are they doing, giving a guy with no experience a light machine gun?*

"Do you know how to use that thing?" I asked Sam.

"I have no idea." At least he was being honest.

These guys had no business being on the front lines and seeing them get weapons issued was disheartening. It made me question if I was in the right place, or with the right unit.

It would be unthinkable for two soldiers to knock on the door of a general's office in the Canadian army—hell, it's unthinkable to talk to a lowly lieutenant on most occasions without going through the chain of command—but our relationship with Araz was different. I felt I had a duty to let the general know what he was taking on in regard to the gang of five.

"These guys are a bunch of clowns and most of them were never in the army." I could see Arman trudging around outside one of the windows. "Look at how fat that guy is," I pointed out for added measure. I wasn't angry, but I could tell Araz was a little surprised. He listened to what we had to say and was even a little sympathetic.

"I know," he said. "I know they are weird, but I'm going to give them a chance."

Fair enough. I wasn't happy, but I had said my piece at least. After that, Araz arranged things so that we were kept apart from Arman's group. That worked for a couple of days, until most of the garrison mounted up for a sizable patrol. Ethan and I loaded up together with Bilal, a good Peshmerga soldier whom we both trusted. So far so good, but then Arman and Mickey hopped in with us. There was an urge to tell them to find a new vehicle, but I checked myself. I was a volunteer in the sense that I wasn't getting paid for what I was doing, but I still wanted to remain professional. Yet it wasn't long before things in the back of the truck began to boil over.

Upon leaving base, Mickey had pulled his skeleton bandana over his face. To the rest of us in the back of the truck, he looked like a goof, but to the civilians we passed on the road the look would have been menacing. We rolled through a town and I could see young children recoiling into their mothers over the sight of the masked man. Enough was enough.

"Show some fucking professionalism and lose that stupid mask."

"It keeps the wind off my face."

"I don't care!" In the military you learn to sound mean and vicious, even if it's just for show. At this moment, however, I was mean and angry and just looking for an excuse to assault the bastard. But he caved quickly enough and rolled the bandana down under his chin. He wasn't happy and neither was Arman, whose mock authority I was probably threatening. I didn't care. There was no love lost between us and I was looking to provoke a fight. Thankfully for them, they kept quiet and we got on with the patrol.

‡‡‡

**16 JANUARY 2015**

"THE SINJAR OPERATION HAS BEEN CALLED OFF." JAMES HAD found me during some downtime on base. He looked dejected. Apparently, Arman couldn't get a chopper. Big surprise.

"Come on, man. You knew that was a bullshit fantasy."

"Yeah, but I hoped—"

"What? You hoped to get helo'd onto a mountain with no chance of a resupply or evacuation? You're ex-military. You're better than that." The American said nothing and looked up to the darkened sky.

"Do you want to die here?" he eventually asked.

*Goddamn it, James.* It's not a topic I wanted to talk about. "Do you?"

"I don't know . . ."

The guy was clearly messed up and I passed him a smoke while thinking of something to say.

"This whole country is at war. If you stay here long enough you'll see battle and when the first bullets fly towards you, you'll know if you want to die." I knew that much to be true.

James smoked the cigarette quickly and asked for another.

"Arman says you got a bunch of men killed in battle. The PKK that you were with at Tal al-Ward."

I had suspected that Arman and Mickey were trash-talking me after the patrol. I have a thick skin, but that was a low blow. Especially coming from people who didn't know the first thing about soldiering and had never been in battle.

"Arman is a fat piece of shit."

What more could I say? A lot, actually, but it wasn't going to be to James. I would take it up with the fat bastard himself.

I made a point of finding Arman the next day. He had his

weapon disassembled and was struggling to put it back together when I confronted him about what James had told me the night before.

"Nah, man. I may have said something that I heard from some other people about a foreigner getting people killed. But no man, I didn't even know it was you that they were talking about." His fat lips were blubbering away the lame excuse when I cut him off by getting uncomfortably close to his face and talking in a quiet voice.

"I have gotten people killed, Arman, a lot of people. But it was with my rifle and a good aim. The next time you trash-talk me, I promise you'll regret it." The man was a weasel and a coward and he said nothing as I walked away. He might have intimidated people back in Germany with his size, bike and gang patches, but in Iraq he was just a loser, playing soldier. Men like that are trouble, though, and they eventually have to be dealt with.


ISIS ARTILLERY BEGAN SHELLING THE KURDISH FRONT-LINE position later that day and by lunchtime everyone was spooled up for battle. Chances are the jihadists were just being pricks, with no other intention than keeping the front-line Kurdish soldiers on their toes, but Araz wanted to hit back with his own heavy guns, and so we mounted up in a convoy of ten trucks. The general always rode in the middle of the convoy and on this day Ethan and I hopped in the rear vehicle with Bilal and another Kurd I didn't know. We checked in on a few artillery and rocket batteries that had already begun counterfiring at the enemy. The rockets howled and whirred. I could never get used to the sounds they made, and in the distance we heard the explosions and hoped that the shells were finding targets.

Just before dusk, our convoy approached one of the big front-line strongpoints, which offered a vantage point of the incoming and outgoing fire. Plumes of smoke rose sporadically from across no-man's-land, indicating where the enemy lines had been hit. The black flags of the Caliphate were barely visible and I remembered the chill that had gone up my spine the first time I had seen the enemy's symbol. I didn't feel that way anymore—the novelty had worn off and I knew the jihadis could be bested on any battlefield.

Coalition planes thundered overhead but released none of their ordnance. *Come on, guys. There are targets everywhere.* I was always disappointed when the various air forces flew away without dropping bombs.

We stayed until it was dark, and then the drivers fired up the engines. Arman and Mickey were lingering around the vehicle I had ridden in, and I watched as Bilal waved them off and pointed them in the direction of another vehicle. They skulked off before Ethan and I hopped back in. As the trucks rumbled away I checked my bag, which had been stowed in the back of the truck, to make sure nothing was missing. I didn't trust Arman or Mickey anywhere near my stuff and with the help of a flashlight I made sure that all my gear was accounted for.

The headlamps of our trucks lit up the sky ahead of us, and along the side of the dirt trail I caught the reflection of animal eyes staring at our procession. About five minutes into our drive, the engine started to cough and sputter. I could hear the driver cursing as it dawned on him that we were running out of gas. I expected the truck to come to an immediate stop, but it carried us over another kilometre and a half of ground before the engine sputtered out completely. Bilal shouted something at the driver, who began flicking the headlights on and off in an attempt to signal the other vehicles in the convoy. But the trucks in front of us kept moving and we watched their lights fade into the night.

Our truck had come to a halt along a remote stretch of the frontier and when the driver cut the lights, the night turned very black. No sense letting the enemy know that there was a lone truck parked in the middle of nowhere. There was a small berm scratched out of the earth that bordered the rough track, but there were no Kurdish bases or soldiers for several kilometres around. We were alone and stranded with nothing but wild dogs for company. At least, we *hoped* there was nothing else lurking in the night.

The fuel gauge was busted, but the driver swore to Bilal that the tank had been filled before we left base. To make matters worse, Bilal's cellphone was dead, so we couldn't get ahold of the convoy, which had long since disappeared. I called Araz's number with my phone and sent him a text, but the general had multiple phones and numbers and there was no response.

I'll admit that being stranded at night while this close to the enemy was scary. If there were ISIS spotters looking at our convoy, we would be in trouble. The jihadis would have seen our truck fall out of the convoy and then known that they had an easy target.

*Arman.* The idea that he was behind our predicament wouldn't leave my mind. What had he been doing around our truck? Had he siphoned our gas, or put a hole in our tank? *Fucking fat bastard.* I would deal with him, but there were more pressing concerns, like what to do now. We were in an exposed position and weighed our options: either walk back to the strongpoint, keep following the track to the next outpost, or stay with the truck. None of the options were great.

Walking to the supposed safety of a Peshmerga outpost carried its own risks, primarily being on the wrong end of some friendly fire. With a lack of communication and it being night, a trigger-happy soldier could easily mistake us for the enemy. Friendly fire is a reality in Kurdistan—it happens often—and I didn't want to take that chance. But staying with the truck carried the risk of being nabbed by the enemy if they had seen us. In the end, we decided to stay with the truck and await help. In the meantime, we took up perimeter positions and stayed alert for the enemy. My greatest fear was hearing the rumble of enemy trucks coming across no-man's-land. If our position were overrun, I would save a final bullet for myself. That's on the mind of every soldier fighting against ISIS. Geneva and its conventions on the rules of war are a long way from Iraq and there's no chivalry in this war, so you're better off taking your own life.

After we'd waited in the cold for an hour, wild dogs started calling out in the night and their eyes reflected off what little moonlight was able to sneak through the clouds overhead. After two hours, I heard what I had been dreading—the sound of an engine rolling over the terrain, and it was getting closer. My heart started to pound and my night vision pulsed with each beat. Beams of light shone over a hill and then came closer and closer to our position. The safety on my gun was off and I waited. We kept to the shadows of the low berm, absolutely still, as two trucks came to a stop. A door opened and a man's voice called out with words I didn't know and Bilal responded, shouting something back.

"Good guys," Bilal said for our benefit. His words hit me with relief.

The trucks had brought several jerry cans of fuel and soon we were on our way back to base. It's funny to think that this was probably the scariest moment of my time in Kurdistan. It wasn't during combat, with bullets zipping inches from my body; the real fear came from being alone on a remote track at night. Maybe it's because there is no time to be afraid in battle—it's more a matter of reacting and letting instincts take over. But I can tell you, being alone on this road at night, close to the enemy, played havoc with my imagination. It was a nightmare, but it was over.

YOU CAN SAY ANYTHING YOU WANT ABOUT ME AND I WON'T GET offended, so long as it's true. Which is why I had a serious problem with Arman's lying and bitter words towards me. I thought I was going to come to blows with the Kurdish-German biker over his trash-talking about me getting people killed at Tal al-Ward, but I had checked myself and in hindsight, that was a mistake. I should have dealt with the bastard then and there. Sometimes the only way to deal with bullies is brute force. I was convinced that Arman had tampered with our truck's gas supply. But my blood was also up because he was still calling into question my conduct in battle.

Arman is a brute of a man. Fat and out of shape though he was, if he ever got his weight behind a punch, he could do some damage. I know a little about this kind of thing and I've definitely been in my share of fights. The last time was in Brandon, Manitoba, when I was stationed with the PPCLI at CFB Shilo. I was coming out of a 7-Eleven store one night and took a shortcut through a dark alleyway. A Native was waiting in the shadows, ready to rob someone. He pulled a knife on me and I reacted quickly by smoking him in the face with my fist. The guy was drunk and stone-cold knocked out when I walked away, leaving him lying on the ground.

But I've also had my ass kicked on the streets of Carleton Place, Ottawa, Edmonton and several places in between and I've learned a few lessons to go along with the beatings that I've been on the wrong end of. Rule number one in fighting: don't be drunk. Rule number two: throw the first punch. I never drank on the front, so rule number one was already taken care of. Now it was time to implement rule number two on the big German-Kurdish bastard. I wanted to give him an ass-kicking.

The door to his Sea Can opened and flooded the immediate area in light and I readied myself. He trundled off to the washroom and then returned a minute or so later.

"Arman!"

He turned and saw my outline in the night. It was too dark to see the expression on my face, but my tone was unmistakable as I marched towards him. My fist was cocked and ready to launch, but now there was more movement in the night. Bilal quickly got between the two of us. He shouted something at Arman and then shoved him hard with both hands. Now it was Arman's turn to raise his fist and as he did, Bilal buried the toe of his boot in Arman's groin. The biker went down and was helped out further with a fist to the face. His considerable weight hit the ground and he let out a groan.

The fight with Arman was over quickly, as all good fights are. Arman hit the ground hard, but he was still conscious. Bilal knelt down beside him, said another few words and then left.

"What did you say to him?" I asked.

"Watch your words."

Arman got the message and for the short while that I remained with General Araz I never had another problem with him. I have no idea if he is still in Iraq, but for the sake of all the good soldiers, I sure hope not.

# 22.

# THE LAST PATROL

MY WAR WAS COMING TO AN END. I DIDN'T KNOW WHEN EXACTLY, but there was an inescapable feeling that my mission was running on borrowed time. There were a couple of factors. First, there was a meeting with Araz. When I was called into his office I initially thought I was in for a dressing-down over the fight with Arman, but that never came up. Rather, the general sat Ethan and me down and had a frank conversation about the pressure the Canadian and American governments were putting on the KRG to release us from service. Araz was adamant about keeping us on the front lines, but there was only so much he could do.

The news was disheartening. When you are risking your life in a war zone, you want to know that your services are wanted and needed. It's sort of like working at a job with the threat of layoffs hovering over your head, except ten times worse. The near-constant threat of being taken off front-line duty since December had been wearing on me. It definitely affected my morale. On top of that, the continued presence of Arman's gang of five was evidence to Ethan and me that perhaps it was time to move on to a different unit. We had both chosen to fight ISIS with the Peshmerga and not the YPG because the Peshmerga was the more professional organization. Yet Arman and the gang of five were putting a strain on this belief. We couldn't trust them, and when you are in battle you *must* be able to trust the guy next to you.

In the Kurdish war against ISIS, there is hardly any cooperation or strategic planning between the Peshmerga and the PKK, but today was a rare exception. General Araz had a meeting with PKK commanders at a small village north of Daquq. The usual complement of vehicles and personnel rolled out of the base at lunchtime and I couldn't help but happily note the absence of Arman and Mickey.

When we arrived at the village of mud and concrete compounds, the PKK were already there and, like usual, they were stirring up the ISIS hornet nest. I was walking on the roof of one of the buildings to get a sense of our location and a better look at the enemy lines across no-man's-land, and with each step I felt my boot squish into the spongy roof that seemed to be made of hay and mud. I don't know how the hell structures like these stay together, but they do. Below I could see a group of PKK fighters with a machine gun mounted on the back of a truck. It was no ordinary machine gun—it looked as though it had been stripped from an aircraft. They had jerry-rigged the firing mechanism and the entire thing was homemade as fuck, yet it worked, and they used the device to sweep the distant enemy lines with gunfire.

That was the way of the PKK. Whereas the Peshmerga were content or disciplined enough to hold their fire between offensive actions, the PKK never missed an opportunity to engage with the enemy, even if it was primarily ineffectual fire from afar. They loved poking at ISIS, who responded with fire of their own. For the rest of the afternoon there were sporadic incoming mortar rounds from the enemy, but thankfully, their aim on this day was off. There were a few close calls, but nobody was hit.

I got down from the roof and took a better look at the machine gun. A German journalist covering the war was doing the same and we said hello.

"Dillon!"

I turned at the sound of my name and saw PKK Ali and his men along a stretch of the berm that guarded the village. There were hugs all around and big smiles on their faces, none bigger than from PKK Ali. I had bumped into his unit a few times throughout my mission and every time it was the same: despite the circumstances of my departure and the fights we had had over my phone and computer, the PKK were always happy to see me. At the end of the day, I had fought alongside them, prevented a nighttime ambush on their base and saved one of their comrades with first aid while under fire, so I guess a lot had been forgiven.

"The PKK never forgets." In different circumstances, these words could easily be a threat. But when spoken by PKK Ali, it was a sign that he and his men would remember the things we accomplished together against the enemy.

James, Juan and Sam were watching. "Does it look like I got a bunch of their friends killed?" I asked James after the hugs and pats on the back were over. He shook his head. "No. I figured Arman was lying about that." I didn't really care what they thought, but now there was proof.

While General Araz met with the PKK in a compound, Ethan and I sat next to the berm. The homemade machine gun was firing and the odd enemy mortar exploded randomly around the village. "Shit, Dillon. I sort of want to join these guys," Ethan said of the PKK. Like me, he knew that our time with Araz was coming to an end and he was looking for options. Plus, he had seen how they treated me and figured they couldn't be that bad.

"It's not worth it, man. They are all smiles and hugs now, but back at their base it's a different story."

"At least I'd see more action." That was true, but still, it wasn't worth it.

"You'd see more combat, but you'd see a lot of other things, too." I had already told him about how I had seen them kill an innocent man and how Hans had had to jump out a window to escape. Then there was the relentless ideological "education" about Marx and communism he would have to deal with. Still, I knew the thought was tempting, but in the end he made the right decision and didn't leave with them.

We smoked and relaxed until General Araz emerged from his meeting and then made our way back to base. As we left, I stole a look at the enemy lines from the back of the truck, and that was the last time I laid eyes on the Caliphate's black-and-white flags.


I'VE MENTIONED ALREADY THAT THE PESHMERGA'S ARMS AND munitions are always critically low despite the fact that the Peshmerga is the only ground force capable of halting the Caliphate's rampage across the desert. The West has been good at delivering air strikes, but what is ultimately needed to defeat ISIS are troops on the ground with the proper weaponry. ISIS has some of the most sophisticated weaponry on the planet, thanks to the American-supplied Iraqi army units, which dropped their weapons and fled in the summer of 2014. To be successful, the Peshmerga needs to be supplied with the same weaponry.

From what I saw in Kurdistan, Germany is the one Western country that has answered the call. I'm not sure what the German affinity is for Kurdistan, but if ever you see sophisticated weaponry in Peshmerga ranks, it's likely from Germany.

A shipment of Carl Gustavs from Germany had arrived at Sheik Jaffer's command centre and General Araz had been summoned to collect his allocation. The Carl Gustav is basically an over-the-shoulder rocket launcher and it's common in NATO armies, including the Canadian military. When an ISIS container truck laden with bombs and oil comes barrelling through no-man's-land, you need something like a Carl Gustav to stop the vehicle before it reaches its target. Small-arms fire from AKs won't do the trick.

Akam was waiting outside one of the main buildings and he waved us over when he saw Ethan and me. He knew we were coming and had been waiting for us. But he wasn't alone. Several American Green Berets were standing nearby, including the guys we had talked to a few weeks earlier at the K1 base. I could tell by the look on Akam's face that he had some news he didn't want to deliver.

"Sheik Jaffer wants to talk to you two, because you have to leave. We are pulling all Westerners out of combat." I knew this day was coming and wasn't entirely surprised by the news. A few days earlier, Ethan had been talking to Akam about joining a different unit, but obviously something had changed.

"We told Sheik Jaffer not to let Americans fight on the front lines," one of the Green Berets said.

"It's a good thing I'm not American," I said.

"Well, you pretty much are," he replied. There was no point getting angry at these guys. Like our previous encounter with the American special forces, this one was friendly and they were nothing but professional. The order to get rid of American fighters was from the U.S. State Department and these soldiers were simply the messengers. The Green Berets were very supportive of what we had done and had a lot of questions about what we had seen at the front, including the enemy activity and the weaponry Araz's unit was outfitted with.

Eventually, Sheik Jaffer stepped outside and, through Akam as an interpreter, thanked us for our service, shook our hands and posed for an official picture. It wasn't my happiest moment, but I was resigned to the fact that my war was over. When we got back to Araz's base, the general called us into his office. Chai Boy brought us all some drinks and emptied Araz's ashtray.

"I want you to stay. Don't worry about Jaffer, it will be okay. Just don't worry and I'll sort things out," the general told us. But how often is a general able to go against his superiors? Not often— it *never* happens.

There was a lot to think about, so Ethan and I talked the situation over in our quarters. I had no doubt that Araz wanted to keep us in his unit, but at the same time we didn't think he would be able to. But there were other considerations too. Even if Araz was able to keep us in country, would it be on the front? With Sheik Jaffer and the KRG breathing down his neck, likely not, and I didn't want to spend my time in the rear echelons, conducting security and training exercises. That's not what I had come here for. I knew that if there was ever another big offensive, we would be held back just enough so that we wouldn't be directly in the shit. When the next Tal al-Ward came, I wouldn't be in the initial rush or on the tip of the spear, charging up the slopes to the enemy positions. I knew what real battle and combat were and I wasn't going to settle into a role where I played at being a soldier from the safety of the rear.

Staying with Araz also meant working alongside criminals, gangsters and sex offenders with no military experience, which also played a role in our ultimate decision to not push back against Jaffer's order. Rejoining the PKK was a nonstarter, but we toyed with some other options, such as joining the YPG or a Christian militia up north. The problem was that we had no connections to the Christian or Yazidi groups fighting in the north and I didn't like the idea of joining the YPG based upon what I had heard from other Westerners as well as their close affiliation with the PKK.

We could have resisted Jaffer's order, but in the end I knew that my initial reason for being in Kurdistan was over. I was disappointed with the overall situation, but there was comfort in knowing I had accomplished what I had set out to do. I had seen combat firsthand, killed the enemy, saved a man's life and made the world a little safer. Warfare is the ultimate test of a man and I knew what I was made of.

When we told Araz we would comply with Jaffer's order, he seemed disappointed. Having two Western veterans in his ranks was a source of pride and added to his renown, but at the same time I'm sure there was a part of him that was relieved that he wouldn't have to defy the order of a superior. We said goodbye to a few of the Kurds we had come to know and then waited with our gear for Lieutenant Ali to pick us up.

Arman's gang saw us waiting with our gear stacked and came over to see what was up.

"What are you guys doing?" they asked.

"Going home," we replied.


AS HE HAD DONE ON SO MANY PREVIOUS OCCASIONS, LIEUTENANT Ali arrived on base to pick us up and then we made the journey to Sulaymaniyah one last time. Lieutenant Ali was disappointed with Jaffer's order to take us off front-line duty and though he tried to persuade me to stay on with the Peshmerga in a logistical or training capacity, he understood why I didn't want to go down that route.

Lieutenant Ali had had my back the entire time I was in Kurdistan, but he had to help me out one final time with my visa before I could leave the country. It's ass-backwards, but in Kurdistan, you can't leave the country unless you have a valid visa. If you arrive at the airport ready to depart without your paperwork in order, you can be jailed and fined. My one-year visa application was with Kurdish intelligence, and Ali had to talk with them so that I could leave the country without being hassled or detained. When it was time, I gave Ali a hug, said goodbye and wished him well. More than anyone else, Lieutenant Ali had made my mission to Kurdistan a reality and after meeting him for the first time, I never once doubted that I had at least one friend I could trust and rely upon for help if need be.

Ali helped Ethan with his departure from Kurdistan as well. Ethan had arrived in Kurdistan with several combat knives, which he hoped to bring back to America. However, a foreigner getting on an airplane with a cluster of knives was bound to raise red flags, so Ali wrote a letter explaining that Ethan had been fighting ISIS and that the knives weren't a threat. Ethan showed the handwritten letter to the security guards at the airport when they saw the blades in his carry-on luggage. They read the letter, apologized for inconveniencing him and then waved him through.

Kurdistan is a fairly remote part of the world, and my flight back to Canada took me first to Qatar and then to London. On my flight to Kurdistan three months before, my mind had been racked by doubt, worry and fear of the unknown. What would happen when I landed? Who would be waiting for me? Was I brave enough to face the enemy on the field of battle? These questions had been answered, but on my flight back home, I realized that there were still so many unknowns that I now had to deal with. What would I now do with my life? Nevertheless, I was more at ease with the knowledge that I had survived the ultimate test of battle and war. I had done what I set out to do, and yet I still wish that I could have achieved so much more. In my mind, I could never have killed enough ISIS fighters, and the thought that I wasn't able to do more gnaws at my soul.

# 23.

# COMING HOME

25 JANUARY 2015
PERTH, ONTARIO
THIS WAS THE SECOND TIME IN FOURTEEN MONTHS THAT I HAD returned to Canada from being at war. After my Afghanistan deployment with the Canadian army, I had arrived home to a warm reception. A military brass band played, dignitaries waited to shake our hands, military officials gave speeches and families hugged and cried after being separated for half a year.

My arrival from Kurdistan could not have been more different.

"Where have you been?" the customs official asked drily at the airport in Toronto, perhaps for the hundredth time that day.

"I was in Iraq, fighting ISIS." It's a unique answer, but the response didn't even faze the bureaucrat sitting behind the counter. He simply carried on with the script.

"Anything to declare?" he asked. I suppose it's possible that he had no idea who or what ISIS is. Or maybe his mind was so numb from doing his job. Regardless, he was a great bureaucrat in the sense that his chief concern was about how many cigarettes I had brought back into the country, rather than the details of my unauthorized armed mission in Kurdistan. It was so typically Canadian. I was thankful, though, because all I wanted to do was get home quickly and the last thing I needed was to be detained by the RCMP.

Before I left Kurdistan, I had touched base with my RCMP contact in Doha and learned that I was on their radar. Apparently, they had a lot of questions for me.

"Just wait till I get home," I told my contact. "Leave me alone at the airport and I'll answer all your questions once I'm back home." That deal was good enough for the RCMP. My sister and my youngest brother picked me up at the airport and we made our way back to my family home in eastern Ontario.

A couple of days later, an RCMP cruiser pulled up the long, icy driveway to the Hillier homestead. My brothers and I had had a few run-ins with the law growing up and this wasn't the first time the cops had paid a visit to the 1840s stone home. But boys will be boys and there were three of us in the family, which caused my parents all kinds of stress and worry. Thankfully, this visit by the police was a little different.

The two RCMP officers, a man and a woman, were friendly and courteous. They always are when they want something from you. The problem was that I didn't really know what they wanted from me. I was concerned and worried that their real intentions might not be so benevolent, and that the real reason they wanted to talk was to gather incriminating information that could be used to prosecute me for going to fight ISIS. Would they nail me for fighting in a foreign war? For killing jihadis? For being with the PKK? I had no idea and they did a poor job of explaining the real reasons why they had made the drive to my parents' place.

It was cold outside, with lots of snow on the ground, but inside the old stone home it was warm and cozy thanks to the woodstove and a pot of hot coffee. We started the interview—or discussion, or interrogation, whatever you want to call it—which lasted for four hours. I was pretty open with the officers, who wanted to know all the minutiae about my time fighting ISIS and how I had come to the decision to fly to Kurdistan.

I also shared a few pictures and videos I had taken in Kurdistan with the RCMP, but there are some videos that I will never show anyone and others that I have deleted because I don't want to remember what the camera captured. They were interested in the images, but eventually the real purpose of the RCMP visit became clear to me: they were looking at my experience fighting with the good guys to better understand how other young Canadians get recruited to fight with the bad guys.

Basically, recruitment boils down to social media. Without Facebook, most of the foreign fighters on either side of the war wouldn't be able to make contacts and probably wouldn't leave Canada to begin with. I know there is a debate about whether Canadian law enforcement should apprehend ISIS sympathizers leaving Canada. In my view, it's much better that Canadian jihadis be monitored but not prevented from leaving for the Middle East. As we saw with the deaths of Warrant Officer Patrice Vincent and Corporal Nathan Cirillo, jihadis in Canada pose a threat to our country. I would much rather these same jihadi converts and radical Islamists travel to the Middle East, where they will first have to pass through a brutal, sexualized initiation rite to get into ISIS, and then be killed in battle. It's an effective way to solve the problem and doesn't cost the taxpayer a dime.

Though the RCMP had been eager to talk to me about my

mission to Kurdistan, it paled in comparison to the eagerness of the media. As soon as word got out that I was back in Canada, requests started flooding in from various media outlets—CNN, CBC and CTV, to name just a few. For a couple of days it seemed like the old stone house was the setting for a movie production, because there were camera crews, light shields, tripods and a steady procession of reporters and journalists everywhere. It was definitely hard to move around the kitchen.

To be perfectly honest, coming home after being in a war zone is a tough adjustment. In hindsight, I should have first spent some time on a warm beach to unwind and destress before coming home. That's a common practice after completing a tour of duty in the Canadian army. After my Afghanistan deployment, my battalion was flown to the Mediterranean island of Cyprus for some rest and relaxation. There was booze and partying, and I can say that beer tastes a lot better than usual when you haven't had a drop for six months. It tastes even better when you are on a beach. The whole point was to unwind in a relaxing environment before coming home to Canada.

The chain of command was especially vigilant about looking out for soldiers displaying signs of post-traumatic stress disorder (PTSD). I sat in on several classes where officers talked to us about the symptoms associated with PTSD, but the vast majority of us were on too much of a high from leaving that Godforsaken country to give our psychological problems much thought. Reliving the bad events of that mission was something that hit me only after I got home to Canada. While having fun in Cyprus, it was easy enough to temporarily bury the guilt and damage I was carrying with me. In fact, I lashed out at and mocked the PTSD instructors and counselors, who I considered were fostering a degrading attitude of victimhood among the men. In hindsight, that was my way of covering up my own mission-related problems. Booze helped with that as well—a little too much, and it eventually led to my being confined to a hotel room and cut off from drinking any more adult beverages in Cyprus.

After seeing so much death and complete savagery in Kurdistan, I wasn't ready to resume a normal civilian life. Even though I had told myself I was fine, my mind just couldn't handle the transition. I sort of felt like I was in a daze.

I'm hesitant to write this, but the truth is that I hit the bottle pretty hard when I got back home. My money was no good at the bars and pubs, with people I had never met offering to buy me drinks at every turn. I did a lot of drugs, too. It was a coping mechanism. Every night I woke up terrified and sweating because in my dreams I had relived men being killed and children screaming for their dead parents. It's an awful feeling and I couldn't get away from it, which is why I self-medicated with drugs and booze. A lot of soldiers suffer this way and it's because we care. On the battlefield I was a killer, but my heart feels for the good people who were lost and the innocents who died.

There's a common saying in the army that your mind is your strongest muscle. Soldiers use those words to remind ourselves that our bodies are stronger and capable of doing more than we think possible. But what do you do when it's your mind that's messed up? That's the problem I had to deal with.

Soon I was at a point where it took all of my effort just to get out of bed and see the sunshine. One morning after a particularly bad night, I broke down and cried uncontrollably for an hour. My mom was there to comfort me as if I were a child. It's embarrassing to say, but I have to let other guys who are messed up from combat know that events like this happen. It was my low point and I needed help.

I found that talking to other veterans who had had similar experiences was the best way for me to make sense of all the strange feelings and emotions I carried with me. A few months after returning to Canada, I was riding on a Via train to Toronto and there was a guy sitting in the seat across from me, talking on his phone loudly enough for me to overhear enough snippets of conversation to realize he had been in the army. It turns out he was a Canadian citizen who was in the marine corps during the second Iraq War. We got to talking, as ex-soldiers do, and though I never mentioned the demons I was battling, this former marine shared some words of wisdom. He had known a lot of people who had killed in combat and every last one of them had turned to booze and drugs afterwards. "I've never known a man not to do drugs and drink way too much after killing someone. Everyone does, but some are never able to pull out and recover."

Killing someone in combat really fucks you up, even if it's for a worthy cause and the people between your iron sights are savages. I took some solace in the man's words, because I wasn't alone in being a mess or in the way that I was dealing with things. I just needed to be one of the guys who recovered. By the time that train ride was over, another soldier who had served in the marine corps joined us. The staff had to tell us to keep quiet. I guess we were carrying on a little too loudly.

Another veteran who helped me put things in perspective is Jody Mitic. I met him at a political event in Ottawa shortly after my return to Canada and I'm glad I did. As a sniper, Jody lost his legs in Afghanistan from a Taliban IED. That would have crushed a lesser man, but Jody carried on and has done some amazing things since his career-ending injury, including getting elected as a city councillor in Ottawa and writing a book, *Unflinching: The Making of a Canadian Sniper*, which you should buy. The man is truly an inspiration and I drew motivation from him. If he could soldier on despite his injury, then I could get my head screwed on straight and conquer my demons.

THE TRANSITION FROM SOLDIER TO CIVILIAN ISN'T EASY OR quick. It's a journey, the length of which remains unknown to me at this time. But I take comfort in knowing that three months in Kurdistan has prevented a lifetime of doubt and wonder about whether I ever made a difference in the world. Was there more to life than the one I was living before? That was the question I started this story with. The answer is a strident yes. Three months in Kurdistan proved that. I will be proud of that time of my life until the day I die.

To be honest, I'm proud that I killed jihadis in Kurdistan. At some level they were men, just like me, but at the same time they were something entirely different. They belonged to one of the most vile and sadistic groups the world has ever known. By carrying arms and fighting under the black-and-white banners of the Caliphate, the fighters I took down had abdicated their humanity in the service of evil. In their hearts, they already knew hell and I'm glad that there are fewer of them walking the earth because of my aim and fire. Maybe one less woman will be raped. Maybe one less child will be butchered because of my actions. I think back on the ruined corpses of the jihadis and I have no remorse. In fact, I sleep easier because of it.

I'm proud that I helped liberate a village and saved a man from certain death. Tal al-Ward is free because of the assault I took part in and Brothahan lived because of the combat first aid I applied. It's a powerful feeling knowing that a man is alive because of me.

I'm also proud that a small number of Westerners have followed in my footsteps to fight ISIS in Iraq and Syria. I showed those who were waiting on the sidelines that it was possible to join the fight and contribute in meaningful ways. Warriors such as Brandon Glossop, a former member of the PPCLI, probably would have gone to fight ISIS anyway, but at least my actions showed the way forward.

But what I'm most proud of is knowing that I did the right thing. War and combat are the ultimate test of a man's character, and I survived. When it mattered most, I didn't back down. I kept my head and allowed my training to take over. Very few will ever know that feeling.

These are the thoughts that I wrap myself in when the going gets tough, when I wake up scared in the middle of the night with the cries of fatherless children wailing in my ears and when the severed heads of men begin to speak. These are the demons and burdens I carry. Everything about war is profound, the good and the bad, and that's the unseen baggage that soldiers carry around. Overall, the bad memories are getting better and are less intrusive, but they still occupy the dark parts of my mind, and something tells me the nightmares will never go away until ISIS is defeated.

Until then, I'll share my story and hope that the war ends quickly. I hope that ISIS is defeated, that the Kurds get their own country and that the screams of women and children are heard no more. Though my rifle is hung up and my boots are untied, I know it's not to be.

# Epilogue

# WINNING THE WAR

WHAT WILL IT TAKE TO DEFEAT THE ISLAMIC STATE? ARE WE
even winning the war? I'm a soldier, not a general, but I've been
asked these questions a lot since my return from Kurdistan and of
course I have a few opinions.

The first thing to understand about ISIS is that it's not simply a terrorist organization, and labelling it as such downplays its
power and strength. In the past, it's been politically convenient
for our leaders to say that our army isn't at war with a particular
country or a people. (We wouldn't want to offend anyone.) It's far
easier for the army brass and politicians to get in front of the flashing cameras and microphones and say we are at war with nebulous
terrorist organizations such as al-Qaida or the Taliban.

Yet ISIS is a de facto state with a semi-functioning government apparatus that can sustain its armed forces in the field. It
has departments of health, education, infrastructure, tax collection
and social welfare as well as utility services. What kind of terrorist organization involves itself in these things? The answer is

none. Osama bin Laden and al-Qaida never cared if the garbage was being collected off the streets of Kandahar or if doctors were being paid in Kabul. That's because al-Qaida was a genuine terrorist organization. But ISIS is different. The Islamic State cares about these things because it's essentially a country, and the Western coalition has to come to terms with this reality if we are actually serious about winning the war. That means setting aside political correctness and admitting that a large swath of the Sunni Muslim population in the region is supportive, or at the very least culpable, in the rise and continued existence of ISIS.

Because ISIS actually controls and administers territory like a real country, it is able to tax its people and sell oil to finance its army. Everybody needs oil, a fact that makes for strange business partners. For instance, the Syrian president, Bashar al-Assad, buys ISIS oil. This gives ISIS the cash it needs to pay its soldiers, who are fighting against the Syrian army. You can't make this stuff up, and it's true that business doesn't care about war and death. Business cares only about buyers, sellers and money.

Once our political and military leadership accept the true nature of ISIS—that it isn't merely a terrorist organization—we can then use our military resources more effectively.

Apart from having a defined geographical region to support and to sustain its forces, ISIS has several other strengths that have to be reckoned with. One of these is that its followers and supporters are fanatically driven with a divine sense of mission and purpose.

When the leader of ISIS, Abu Bakr al-Baghdadi, rose to the podium at the al-Nuri mosque in Mosul and declared a caliphate in June 2014, he was sending a message to all Muslims around the world. The ancient Islamic Caliphate was reborn and he was its leader. By evoking the resurgence of the Caliphate, al-Baghdadi had raised the stakes in global jihad. Under his watch, ISIS isn't just some two-bit terrorist organization content on kidnapping foreign nationals and blowing up embassies, like al-Shabaab or the various al-Qaida splinters around the world. Rather, would-be jihadis look to ISIS as a force of historical destiny that will fulfil the prophesies of the Quran and establish Islamic order throughout the entire world. In the world of jihad, this is big stuff.

It's this sense of historical mission and destiny that gives ISIS what Sun Tzu called the "Moral Law" when he wrote *The Art of War* over two thousand years ago. Sun Tzu's Moral Law has nothing to do with right and wrong, but it has everything to do with men following their leaders without any regard for their own personal safety. This explains the mentality of the ISIS fighters. They are willing to follow the commands of their leaders, even if it means blowing themselves up in a suicide mission or launching forlorn attacks with little chance of success.

It's no secret that in addition to making stunning territorial gains, ISIS has also absorbed stunning casualties in battle. Virtually every Canadian that has gone to fight for the Caliphate has been killed in combat or air strikes. I'm sure the figures are similar for nationals from other countries too, and yet foreign recruits continue to pour into and replenish the jihadist ranks despite knowing the strong likelihood that they too will be killed. Such is their fanaticism and the lure to jihad. The enemy fighters are driven by the historical mission and destiny that ISIS has to offer, and that is the Moral Law in action. It's what makes ISIS such a fanatical and inhuman foe.

Man for man, ISIS fighters are terrible compared to NATO-trained soldiers. But it's not that kind of war. It would be over soon if it were. Yet when matched up against the Iraqi army—or even the Kurdish Peshmerga—the Islamic jihadis have proven their effectiveness in battle. A lot of their success comes from simply having better morale. In other words, it's their will to fight. The jihadis are willing to fight and die for their cause whereas the Iraqi army is more often than not prepared to run away and abandon its weapons. Just like horses and water—you can lead the Iraqi army to battle but you can't make it fight.

So a willingness to fight is the first ingredient for a successful army, and ISIS unfortunately has that. It also has decent tactics and military know-how. There are lots of examples throughout history of smaller nations defeating larger nations through rapid movement and surprise attacks. Hitler and the German army nearly pulled off the greatest surprise attack of all time when they turned their guns east on the sleeping Russian bear in the 1941 Blitzkreig.

ISIS launched its own blitzkrieg in the summer of 2014, when it spilled out of Syria and rolled up large portions of Iraq, including the city of Mosul. Surprise was the key. No one expected its lightning advance and everyone was caught off guard. Even the Kurdish Peshmerga was pushed back. ISIS essentially doubled its territory in the span of a few months. A mere terrorist organization could never have pulled off such a campaign. The logistics and planning required for a campaign like this are huge, which shows the level of organization and sophistication that the Islamic State possesses. It also helps that a number of Saddam Hussein's former generals have lent their experience and expertise to the Islamic State's army.

Whether it's Iraq or Afghanistan, suicide bombings have always been the bane of Western soldiers fighting against jihadis. Unfortunately, ISIS has taken the concept of the suicide bomber and put it on steroids. Anti-personnel and anti-vehicle IEDs are still used, but the real danger is posed when a drugged-up ISIS member explodes a tanker truck full of oil along the front lines. Unless the truck is destroyed before it reaches its target, nothing can be done. The explosion destroys everything and creates mass confusion and punches a hole in the defensive lines. The jihadis then exploit the newly formed gap and start attacking the flanks and rear of their opponents. Admittedly, it's an effective tactic.

Though some territory has been regained from ISIS, mostly by the Kurds, the jihadis have been pretty good at digging in and defending their gains. Their defensive works and trenches are adequate, they take advantage of natural defences and they have no problem mining the shit out of cities and towns to deter attacks.

The ISIS commanders have also shown some military wisdom by not fighting important battles that they know they will lose. When the Iraqi army and Shia militias eventually got their act together to retake the small city of Tikrit, ISIS fought a rearguard action, which delayed their enemies. Meanwhile, they shifted forces to the south and captured the even more significant city of Ramadi.

I've already written a few times about how ISIS has sophisticated weaponry, but it's worth repeating and it's all because of the incompetent Iraqi army. The United States has spent billions trying to create, train and equip an effective Iraqi army, and of course it's money well wasted. Huge stockpiles of modern military hardware fell into the hands of ISIS when the Iraqi army melted in front of Mosul. Guns, artillery, mortars, recoilless rifles, munitions, night vision goggles and even tanks are all part of the ISIS arsenal.

Psychological warfare is as old as warfare itself. Hannibal used

African elephants to scare the crap out of the legions of Rome, and the real-life Dracula earned the nickname "the Impaler" for, you guessed it, impaling Ottoman troops on wooden stakes. (Coincidentally, ISIS does this too.) Fear is the common factor and you can't talk about the Islamic State without mentioning it. The first time I saw the black-and-white flags of ISIS, I was scared. Even though they were far away, a chill went up my spine because I knew what they represent. We've all seen ISIS's sadistic videos, in which captives are executed in the most brutal and inhuman ways. Yes, it's done partially because the jihadis are animals. But it's also a calculated propaganda ploy meant to strike fear into their enemies.

And it works. Every time I faced off against ISIS, a part of me remembered what my fate would be if I was captured. Without question, I would have killed myself before being taken prisoner. A bullet to the head would be far easier than being taken captive, and everyone I met on the front felt the same way. One of my greatest fears was being wounded and incapacitated to such a point that I wouldn't be able to pull the trigger if need be. I was able to shove the fear of the enemy to the side and focus on soldiering, but that can be debilitating for some men. I've seen some Kurdish soldiers crack and lose their minds because of combat stress, and a good part of that was rooted in fear.


THERE YOU HAVE IT. ISIS IS BASICALLY A REAL COUNTRY THAT can finance a long war. It has fighters who believe in the cause, decent tactics and modern weaponry and it has scared the shit out of its enemies.

So what can be done about it?

Quite a bit, actually.

Like I said before, the individual soldiering skills of ISIS fighters are a notch above shit. That's good enough for the region that they are in, but if Western troops ever engaged them in battle, they would fold. At Tal al-Ward I fought against ISIS's elite fighters. We charged up a hill against an entrenched enemy, fully exposed and under fire the entire time, and we still kicked their ass.

In my honest opinion, if Canada turned the PPCLI loose in Iraq, the war would be over in a month. There would be casualties, but we would win. I'm not saying that's the best option, only that if we are serious about winning the war, it can be done.

I don't think there is much appetite to send American, British or Canadian troops into Iraq, and frankly that's not needed anyway. The Kurdish and Iraqi soldiers are already on the ground and all they need is the proper support to even the odds. What we need to start doing is arming the Kurdish Peshmerga directly. Right now, most Western weaponry destined for Kurdish forces goes through Baghdad first. Of course, some goes "missing" along the way and there are Iraqi officials making a fortune on the black market. It's a disgrace.

Iraqis, whether they be Sunni or Shia, mostly hate the West. That includes Canada. The Kurds, on the other hand, love the West. After the Israelis, they are the most tolerant, liberal and pro-Western people in the region and we should be supporting them directly with the weapons they need: guns, munitions, they need it all. This isn't the time to be cheap. I feel like our country is being hypocritical and condescending when we pat the Kurds on the back and tell them what a great job they are doing fighting ISIS, but then we don't back up our words with tangible weapons support.

Another thing the West can begin doing immediately is to use our overwhelming air power more effectively. I forget how many online news reports I read while in Kurdistan about Canadian planes flying sorties without dropping any bombs. It angered me every time. During every stint along the front, I could look out across no-man's-land and see enemy flags and activity. *They are right there*, I would say to myself, and yet there were apparently no targets to bomb from the air.

It's just not true. There are lots of targets to hit. What there isn't enough of is the political courage to do what needs to be done. If there is an artillery piece set up beside a mud hut, we need to blow it up. If there is a tank in the middle of a village, we need to destroy it. If there is an enemy trench system on the edge of a town, we need to bomb it. Yes, the bleeding hearts will cry out and there will be collateral damage. But this is a war, not a walk in the park. People are going to get killed and it's either going to be jihadis or our allies doing the dying. The choice to me is pretty clear: we need to turn our pilots loose and let them do their job, which is dropping bombs. General Sherman was right when he said that war is cruelty and the crueller it is, the sooner it will be over. Every day that ISIS exists is a day that more civilians will be killed and more migrants drowned in the sea as they try to escape the Caliphate.

If I had it my way, Western planes would unleash an unprecedented aerial bombing campaign of the jihadi capital of Raqqa in Syria. This city is the epicentre of ISIS's strength, power and administration. Without Raqqa, ISIS cannot function as a de facto country. Its economic system will collapse and it won't be able to support its armies in the field. A campaign against Raqqa would also send a message to the thousands of people in that city who regularly turn out to witness ISIS's staged executions, baying like mad dogs for the blood of their enemies. It may sound cruel or callous, but I really don't have much sympathy for these people. We have a tendency in the West to fight wars with one arm tied behind our backs, but in the long run, such hesitation only makes things worse.

FINALLY, I WOULD BE REMISS IF I DIDN'T SAVE A FEW WORDS for the role of Western volunteers like me. I was lucky in the sense that I was the first volunteer with the Peshmerga and so I got to see action on the front lines. Unfortunately, the days of foreign volunteers seeing trigger time on the front with the Peshmerga are over; they are restricted to rear-echelon duties such as support and training. This may not be as glamorous as battling the jihadis face to face, but it still serves a useful purpose. Western veterans have a wealth of tactical experience they can use to teach the Kurdish soldiers to make them better fighters. There are a lot of basic skills that every Canadian or American veteran has, like first aid, proper firing techniques and manoeuvring skills, that would help in the fight against ISIS. Instead of sending out mixed messages about possible repercussions for foreign volunteers, the government should be clear that going overseas to fight ISIS is not against the law. I'm not saying Ottawa needs to support or encourage those who go over, but at the very least it should be neutral about this activity.

I think there are a lot of brave Canadian veterans with military skill sets that could make a difference but who are sitting on the sidelines because they don't want to be hassled by their own government. I even have army friends who were on their way to

Kurdistan to join the fight but were stopped at the airport and prevented from going any farther. This shouldn't happen. The men who can make a difference should be allowed to contribute in the fight against evil. Heck, maybe the government could even spot them their airfare.

ISIS HAS BEEN ABLE TO MARAUD ACROSS SYRIA AND IRAQ because of some brilliant early victories. But it isn't invincible and we could win the war in a month or two. It would be messy and dirty and lethal, but with an intensification of air strikes and more material support to the Kurds, ISIS can be defeated. I can think of no greater gift to humanity and civilization. That's my two cents, but I'm not a general. I'm just a soldier, and the first volunteer.

# ACKNOWLEDGEMENTS

DECIDING TO WRITE THIS BOOK WAS THE HARD PART. FROM the beginning, we decided that if we were going to tell this story, it had to be authentic and real, complete with the good and the bad. We weren't interested in sugarcoating anything and the truth of what happened in Iraq isn't pretty. The question became: Could we stand by the truth of war, or would the fallout be too much to handle? We made our decision and this book is the answer.

We want to thank our agent, Linda McKnight from Westwood Creative Artists, for seeing the potential of this book early and finding a great publisher and editor to work with us. We owe a big thanks to Jim Gifford with HarperCollins, who did a fantastic job editing the book with his expertise and wise counsel.

Thank you to Julien Frechette and member of provincial Parliament Patrick Brown for your insights and meaningful contributions. Thanks as well to friends and colleagues Ashley Rydahl and James Cousin for all the words of encouragement. It meant a lot.

To the over two hundred Canadians who donated money to help buy night vision goggles for the fight against the Islamic State, you know who you are. You are the example and you made a difference. Your generosity won't be forgotten.

Thanks, Jess, for putting up with my writing over several months. Can you hang in for one more?

Finally, thanks, Dad, for all the support and the many times you read and reread the manuscript.

Dillon and Russell Hillier